PRAISE FOR DIRT CHURCH

"Charity's unique story, shifting from a worldview of separation formed in her through a fundamentalist version of Christianity, to the reality of our interconnection with the whole alive world, is courageous, touching and relatable. Although her story is her own, it is also universal. She speaks to the heart of a movement from institutionalism and control into experiential relationship with nature and with others from a place of reverence and love for the 'other,' and mutual belonging. She covers a wide field from sexuality to empathy, technology to spiritual healing. Readers are led on a particular and collective journey in rewilding, inviting them to reflect on their own lived experiences. At this time in human history, with a metacrisis and a planet in peril, we need authentic stories like Dirt Church that open up space to re-imagine and re-wild the way things are. We need community experiences that invite others in, as Charity has, that intersect with a new and ancient spirituality that I witness blossoming in the Wild Church Network. You'll be glad you opened this beautiful book."

— VALERIE LUNA SERRELS, CO-FOUNDER/MYCELIAL WEAVER, WILD CHURCH NETWORK

DIRT CHURCH

DIRT CHURCH
ANSWERING THE CALL TO REWILD SPIRIT

CHARITY MUSE

Cover artwork and cover design: Cass Combs

Print ISBN: 979-8-9861031-3-6

eBook ISBN: 979-8-9861031-4-3

To Willow & Sycamore: May you always remember you are sacred and wild and that this Earth is your Mother.

———

To all of those who've found themselves in a different place spiritually: May you unearth your own sacred wild being.

CONTENTS

CHAPTER I
RETURNING TO DIRT

> *The world is charged with the grandeur of God;*
> *It will flame out, like shining from shook foil.*

— GERARD MANLEY HOPKINS

WHEN I STARTED WRITING this book, I did not realize the journey I was about to be led on. Sitting on a blanket in my backyard in northern Georgia, underneath Grandmother Pecan tree, I heard a gentle whisper in my heart.

Write a book called Dirt Church. Rewild yourself.

What I thought would happen was that I would write a book on finding God in the wilderness. What actually happened pushed me beyond the edges of what I thought I knew—into a wider, wilder, and deeper view of Spirit and love for this planet than I could have imagined that afternoon gazing at the sky through the limbs and leaves.

Perhaps being the granddaughter of a Pentecostal pastor predisposed me to be attuned to the spiritual realm. Perhaps being a Cancer sun and rising and a Pisces moon magnifies my

1

sensitivity. Perhaps being an Enneagram Four makes me see things differently, and makes me more readily able and willing to dive into the depths of thinking and emotion, into the something-we-can't-see-or-touch.

Whatever the reason, there has been a consistent thread of knowing, trusting, and believing throughout my life. Even though they somehow come easily to me, there is a sense of something just out of reach—evasive, and like the bird you can hear in the tree, but never locate with your eyes.

In a similar way, I've always been drawn to the trees, the earth, the soil—relishing in the scents of pine and fallen leaves as I walk the paths along mossy banks in the forests I visit. In ways I can't explain, I have often had the experience of being held in these spaces, even having a sense of *knowing that I belong* at the loneliest moments of my life when circumstances and external voices have most convinced me that I don't. The threshold of the wild has called me back to myself and returned me to the sanctuary of my soul.

No matter where I travel, the smell of the river brings a sense of home and the sight of mountains a reminder of where I belong. Perhaps, from all the time I spent at my grandparents' home near the Tennessee River in Chattanooga, TN. Or I listened to too much John Denver in my youth.

Or maybe it's a call deeper than the one I can hear with my ears. Perhaps I have been hearing the voice of Spirit in the wild places.

From the hawks crying as they circle hundreds of feet overhead in the updrafts to the microbes below the soles of our feet, life is teeming everywhere. There is no place where the Divine is absent.

After my daughter's third grade field trip, I listened to the podcast "On Being" on the way home, and the guest talked about the wilderness as the place he was cast out to after walking away from evangelical Christianity. He went on to compare this experience to one of danger and pain.

Something in me tensed up. I immediately recognized that this is not my experience as a queer southern woman who has also left evangelicalism. On further reflection, I pinpointed that my discomfort was rooted in the fact that I no longer identify with the metaphor of wilderness as the place where we are alone. I no longer see the wilds as a place of threat or lack. Instead, I am captivated by the Source in all things around me. Instead, I see the wilderness as an invitation to connect with Divine Mystery. It is the *Sacred Wild*.

The truth I've found is that the more I engage with what has been vilified by the Western church—the wilderness and natural world, my own wildness, and spirituality outside of the confines of dogma—the closer I feel to Spirit. The more I awaken to how deeply connected I am to all that is, the further I am freed from institution and authoritarianism, including that within the church.

And when I pay attention, I see this manifestation of Spirit everywhere. Red deadnettle forces itself through the thick layer of dead grass in the off-season hay field. Blue jays tap their beaks on the upper pecans remaining in the tree in early January. Two young deer graze in the distance, wary of my presence. All of this sings to me like a sacred hymn.

I now see the wilderness as not just a place beyond margins, but *the* place where Spirit is most tangible, and where we are most receptive to Her. I've come to know the Creator through the beauty and wildness in nature herself, and through this clarity, I see the abundance and safety all around. Unlike the pavement we've poured over hallowed ground, the artificial lights, and the walls we've carefully constructed, the untamed wilderness is home. Where we live, and move, and have our being.

It would be all too easy to assume that what I am suggesting is that the metaphor of wilderness for difficulty or aloneness doesn't work. However, that's an overly simplistic view that obscures a much deeper and more needed insight. As you join me in this journey along these pages, you'll see the wilderness, both metaphorical and literal, is where we actually find what we often call God, the Divine, Spirit, Divine Mystery. I believe when we offer ourselves to the Wilds and engage with the unbroken-ness and untamed-ness of it all and open ourselves to learning, we connect with ourselves, the world, and Divine Source most deeply.

In our current time, especially for those of us who were raised in fundamentalist traditions or who have experienced spiritual trauma, there seems to be a choice placed before us to either remain in beliefs we've long held onto, or to burn it all down to the ground. While anger and pain might fuel us to choose the latter or fear might urge us to grip on ever tighter to what we've known, neither of these choices leave much room for growth, further connection, or soul journey.

But a third way beckons us to weigh our beliefs and values, closely examine ourselves, and reform spiritual identity in a way that's authentic to ourselves and what we believe. We are beckoned to do it in the context of community and along with the natural world. In no other place have I better learned how to do this or been more inspired to continue to go deeper than in the Sacred Wild.

———

THE CANOPY of trees offer themselves to us, whispering that there is a knowing we can reach if we will listen with our whole bodies.

The birds offer insights to our ears and echo a call to listen more deeply, from our hearts.

The rivers and streams offer healing and baptism into deeper connection and understanding of the rivers flowing under the rivers. They clue us in to the nature of Spirit at work.

This book offers itself to you as a path into the beauty of the *Sacred Wild* and *our own wildness*. I like to imagine we are walking together, and I'm showing you some of my favorite wonders and what I'm learning. You may notice your own insights as we journey along.

In addition to resources and suggested readings at the end of the book, there are embodied eco-spiritual practices included at the end of each chapter. You are going to be asked to go outside. I encourage you to recognize that there is no bad weather, only bad clothing. Too often, we stop ourselves from going outside because of discomfort. If there is truly severe weather, simply wait.

You are going to be asked to roll up your sleeves and get to work. I encourage you to do the practices and to journal about them as you go along. I encourage you to write (by hand if possible) what you are thinking and feeling. You might be surprised at what comes out.

Even moreso, I encourage you to go through this book with other people. Or at the very least, include someone else in some of the practices and discuss them together. Part of separating ourselves from institutionalism and reconnecting with our wildness is to reject our obsession with individualism and return to community. As you read, you will also see my deep belief that this is an important dimension of spirituality which we have long neglected and must return to. This is not about an individualistic spiritual practice. It's far past time we move away from those models which encourage the personal or transcendent over the communal. Commune with others, commune with more-than-humans and nature, and commune with Spirit/Source as you read this book.

WHILE THIS BOOK is not a theological debate or a replacement for professional service or guidance, it is an invitation.

I invite you to *shift*—to shift into action, to reconnect to Spirit. I invite you to grow your love and connection with the Sacred Wilderness and the wild within you. So we may save our wild spirits and also the wilds of the world.

I am not a climate activist in the professional sense of the word, but I care deeply and work for conservation. I love this Earth as my mother. From a very early age when I started a chapter of Kids Save Earth (KSE) with my best friend Stephanie in elementary school, to now in my forties, I am committed to saving what we can. Though I'm not a scientist or activist by trade, I can say with confidence: The Earth needs us to wake up. Our beautiful amazing planet regenerates and rewilds herself faithfully, but for full restoration, we need to get out of the way and start to live and love differently.

Many of us have lost our soul connection with our Mother the Earth, with Source, with our true selves. I believe love will heal us. Love will heal our bond and begin to heal the wounds we've inflicted on our home and on ourselves.

As we embark on this journey together, I invite you to take a deep breath in, and imagine your heart opening to contain the multitudes of be-loved ones here around us now. The sky, the waters, the mountains and deserts and forests and plains, and all life within. No creature too small or place too far gone. Imagine your heart now open to love, to befriending and to the restoration of relationship and kinship long forgotten. From this place, we will go into the sacred wildness of Dirt Church.

CHAPTER 2

CHURCH AND DIRT

> *No wonder the hills and groves were God's first temples, and the more they are cut down and hewn into cathedrals and churches, the farther off and dimmer seems the Lord.*

— *JOHN MUIR*

WHEN I THINK of my history with church and spirituality, it surprises me that I would gravitate to finding the Divine outside of the boundaries and prescriptions of church and religiosity. Growing up as the granddaughter of a Pentecostal pastor in Chattanooga, TN, church mandated the details of our everyday being. Our entire week revolved around the church schedule. My family members taught Sunday school, led the choir or sang in service, played instruments, or performed some other function within the church. Even after my grandfather left that church, my family stayed within the Pentecostal denomination, and our lives continued to orbit around our new church and our involvement there.

At that time in my life especially, I defined church as a building as well as a lifestyle and culture. In some ways, church offered community, but only with the people who showed up regularly and lived in line with the ways that we interpreted the Bible. That way of thinking continued to permeate my mind as I became a teenager and found myself immersed in what I now recognize as religious fundamentalism which found its way into both our politics and everyday vernacular.

I not only bought into the youth group ideologies of the 1990s, I was the poster child for being "radically saved" with my Christian t-shirts and WWJD bracelets. I formed a Christian rock praise and worship band for my youth group, helped start a Bible study at my high school (because Fellowship of Christian Athletes wasn't Christian enough for me!), and held a leadership role in my youth group.

But for what I gained in apparel and even skills in music and leadership, I paid a steep price in self-abandonment, especially my own wildness.

I grew afraid of my own sexuality, desperately trying to pray the gay away in secret and isolation, even though I had known I was attracted to girls since I was six years old. By the time I was 12 and throughout my adolescence, I hid most of myself in shame. Many nights, I lay flat on the floor of my bedroom in the dark, crying and praying that God would somehow change me and terrified I would go to hell. I didn't dare tell anyone about my secret other than sharing vague notions that I was "struggling," for fear of being found out. So, I listened to Melissa Etheridge and the Indigo Girls while daydreaming about what life could be like during the day but cried myself to sleep at night. I felt as though I would never be wholly accepted unless God somehow changed me.

In high school, especially, the pressure to be more separate from the world became greater. Though I adored many musical artists in the mid-late 1990s, I became deeply wary of the potential influences of secular music, so I faithfully broke many of my CDs. I started worrying that watching TV shows and movies with gay characters might lead me or others down the wrong path. I bought into the notion that it was harmful to have friends who were not also believers in the God I worshipped—the God I was taught would punish us and banish us away if we fell short of perfection.

This line of thinking permeated Christian culture, resulting in an explosion of contemporary Christian music, Christian education, and a slew of Christian brands for everything from financial advice to dieting and self-help. Everywhere I looked offered confirmation that I was on the right path to completely deny myself and take up the cross if I wanted to belong to Jesus and belong with his followers. Separate from the world. Sold out. Radical.

Thankfully, I didn't stay there.

Though more time has passed since the 1990s than I would care to admit, not much has changed in how this line of thinking dominates discussions and thought within the Western Church. Perhaps it has gotten even worse, and the rhetoric has become more fear-based, hateful, and further from the teachings of Jesus himself.

I have come to realize that not just the doctrine of separation, but a vilification of wilderness and wildness permeates Western Christian thought. For those of us who challenge the status quo by our very existence (queer, neurodiverse, women, etc.) this presents a particularly difficult challenge. The dominating church norm has become sterilized and hostile toward anything different or other, sometimes even in places which proclaim they are affirming or progressive.

Worship songs have often become formulaic and distant from the experiences of everyday living. Traditional heavy-handed hymns and patriarchal empirical language find their way into words sung and spoken. Unofficial dress codes, "us and them" attitudes and language, exclusionary website statements of faith, rigid gender roles, and strict views on sexuality all normalize a culture of wildness-suppression. It isn't that these practices are necessarily new, but in this current moment, they seem more pronounced, and, frankly, more dangerous than ever.

Even within more progressive churches, orders of service often prescribe the elements of gatherings, and even when we are expected to sit or stand. Songs are often filled with archaic imperial language, outdated tunes and rhythms, and singing is frequently relegated to the few who have been "properly trained." This leaves little room for creativity, spontaneity, and the Wild Divine to dance among us.

In the sterilization, colonization, and taming of spirituality, we have come to fear what we were once comfortable with and what once provided safety. We instead have become comfortable with what should terrify us.

In migrating ourselves and our spiritualities to carefully curated and constructed indoor spaces, we insulate ourselves and become soft (acquiescent, neutral, too comfortable), where we should be tough and resilient. Meanwhile we have hardened our hearts and minds where we should remain soft, gentle, open, and curious.

Instead of seeing home, safety, community, and shelter for wildlife in the trees, we see profit, potential, or even danger. Instead of seeing medicine and food in the wild plants growing in our yard and gardens, we see "weeds" and encroachment on manicured monoculture lawns and fields.

So we turn to the saw, the logging trucks, the chemicals, and heavy machinery. We cozy ourselves up to corporations and agencies hell-bent on capitalistic gain at the steep cost of choking our planet.

In the same manner, instead of seeing community, connection, and belovedness in each other, we see danger and potential enemies. Instead of seeing medicine for the loneliness epidemic and food for the soul in wildness and spontaneity, we see threat to order in our selective (often white, cis-heteronormative, neurotypical), overly organized, and tamed ideas of spiritual community.

So we turn to the excluding statements of faith, unimaginative liturgies and songs, and the same genres of music we are prescribed and conditioned to use. We cozy ourselves up to hierarchy, talking heads, political parties, and influencers hell-bent on capitalistic gain at the steep cost of choking out love and liberation from the church supposedly modeled after Jesus, the teacher of peace, love, justice, interconnectedness, and mercy.

We trade plowshares and pruning hooks for warcraft and assault rifles. We sacrifice the collective good and tending the earth on the altar of a vague and ill-defined idea of "freedom" that translates to empire and oppression, violence and death.

To add insult to injury, this spills over into our daily lives as we "connect" through technology. We place a screen between each other and manage our feeds and lists to only include accounts we agree with and see eye-to-eye on. We are careful with what we share: filtered images and words. We've tied our hands and let our muscles of discourse, peacemaking, and navigating conflict atrophy into the visceral fat of engaging *only* what is easy, surface, and effortless.

How DID WE GET HERE?

When I look back on the teachings many of us experienced in the Western Church, I notice a common thread. Throughout lessons, books, songs, and more, we are admonished to be separate from the world, and to fear the world around us. At minimum, we are taught to be skeptical of the world and to learn to control nature around us.

Is it not possible that the imperialization of Christianity and accompanied mistranslations and misunderstandings created many of these chasms between nature and humanity, as well as separations within ourselves?

We are told to take dominion over the world and use it for our gain, disregarding and de-personifying nature. Patriarchal language and whiteness favor capitalism, industry, and what can be controlled over wildness and cooperative living. And as we know too well, those messages are strongly reinforced by western ideals of success and power. As colonizers took over the land, they also warped and distorted an interdependent faith and way of living into a religion of empire and dominance.

To love or be one with the world is equated to being an enemy of God. The doctrine of separation of church and the world scolds those of us who would immerse ourselves into nature and speak of the wonders of finding Spirit there. This deeply ingrained dogma limits our understanding and perspectives and maintains strict sterility—until the natural world comes crashing into the church in a way that can no longer be ignored or shut out.

My friend Claire once served as an Episcopal priest in downtown Chattanooga. In September 2020, her church held an outdoor worship service like so many congregations did around that time because of COVID safety precautions. While Claire preached a sermon, a black bear ran through the parking lot, prompting worshippers to yell "bear!" during an Episcopal church service where, unlike in my Pentecostal upbringing, yelling is *not* the norm.

I asked Claire about this recently. Unsurprisingly, she had been alarmed and found humor in the bear, like many of the parishioners present. Looking back, she still finds it surreal, and reflects on the potential lessons of urbanization of areas that were once wild, encroaching more and more on the habitat of other lives. She wisely offers insight that this may have been a strange convergence of being open to something new in the midst of the pandemic.

What captivates me the most is the topic of her sermon that evening, based on Exodus 17: "Is the Lord among us or not?"

Part of me can't help but ponder on the idea of Divine in the bear. Creator in the meeting of power and wildness with ritual and gathering. Spirit in the intersection of safety precautions and social distancing with peril and closeness, too close for many. Divine Mystery is already present, yet we ask the question if Spirit is here. Like Jacob, we are waking up and wondering.

In her book, *Mating in Captivity*, couples therapist, author, and erotic intelligence expert Esther Perel suggests that the ways we diminish ourselves in our relationships in order to provide more safety and security actually harm us and invite more danger into our relationships. I think the same is true in spirituality and our own wildness. The more we tame ourselves and diminish our wildness and connection to the Sacred Wild, the more imperiled our spirituality becomes. It lacks the core essence that makes it viable: *wild life.*

To engage with the wilderness is to accept that there is risk. When we embark on returning to our own wildness, we acknowledge the uncertainty of not only where this will lead us, but also *how this will change us.* Once we move forward, there is no going back. There is no return to the carefully constructed "safety" of racial injustice, patriarchy, classism, and imperialism married with religiosity and fundamentalism. Nor can we return to our carefully constructed illusions of safety in the boxes and barriers we have mistaken for normalcy.

Instead, we are invited to recognize the dangers of complacency, insulation, and routine. We are liberated from the narratives and societal norms we have internalized by suppressing our own spirits. As we walk among the trees and find ourselves caught up in the fragrant forest and feel the power of rushing waterfalls, we begin to hear our own voice and tremble at the holy reckoning with our truest selves—the selves most connected with each other, with the Earth, and with Spirit.

In the Christ tradition, there is a story around the miracle of the resurrection. Women who knew and loved Jesus went to tend to his body after he had been laid to rest. When they arrived to find the tomb empty, they were troubled and a stranger said to them, "Why do you seek the living among the dead?"

It seems to me that for much of the history of Christianity, and even today, we have continued to seek the living God, the Great Mystery, Spirit, among the dead.

Christianity in its empirical form has been extensively used as a tool of oppression, violence, death, and destruction toward both humans and the planet.

But the living is not found in control or hate or tyranny. Nor is Spirit found in the dead trees and stones that have been stolen from their rightful places and carved, hewn, and shaped by humans into forms meant to serve human purposes. Church buildings, chairs, pews, pulpits, and offering baskets bear little resemblance to their original living being.

To paraphrase the quote at the beginning of this chapter

from naturalist John Muir, this misuse dims Spirit and separates us from Her.

Why do we continue to seek a Divine who shows up in a barn, in the voice of a donkey, in fire, in wind, in the sea, on the sea, in a dove, in the margins, in the outcasts, in the oppressed, in the protests, in the dirt, in the garden, and in the wilderness itself... in our carefully constructed boxes? Why would we believe Spirit would inhabit *anything but* wildness and liberation and the poor and oppressed?

When church and therefore so much of spirituality has been designed for control, curation, and comfort, wildness clearly can have no place there. I learned that the hard way even while writing this book, when I was forced out of my worship leading role and my progressive church for my own untamed-ness. (Change the lyrics to the wrong hymn to make it more inclusive, and you will make enemies!)

But when a spiritual community is open to creativity, diversity, and cultivating space, hope, and goodness, the open invitation to wildness stands to transform our communities into vibrant oases and groves in a world increasingly thirsty and hungry for connection, belonging, and love.

Perhaps the best place to begin the work lies within remembering where we came from, and the potential we still hold within our sacred wild selves.

INVITATION

Take a pen and paper (or journal) outside. Notice what you hear and what you see when you sit in silence for a few moments. Then, reflect on the following questions:

In what ways have you felt your own wildness suppressed by the church? (or if that is not your experience, you may wish to substitute another institution such as a particular school, a workplace, etc.)

In what ways have you witnessed or even participated in wildness suppression in your environment?

How have you tamed yourself? What wants to be released to be wild within you?

CHAPTER 3
REMEMBER

When I step out into the grey of the early morning, I join in the silence and reverence for what's about to happen. I know that soon, the sky will begin to change, but for now I can still see the bright glow of the full moon. The dark, as I've learned, is the beginning. From the ashes and from the silence, the birds will come to life. The sun will crest over the horizon, causing the sky to sing with colors and vibrance. The dew will begin to sparkle, and if I am still for long enough, I can remember this is the beginning of all things.

It's no mistake that so many spiritualities and scientific theories contain a creation or origin story of how Earth came to being. In the beginning, we remember most clearly who and what we are. In our origins, we get in touch with our aliveness, our brokenness, and our wholeness. Through remembrance, we offer ourselves the chance to right what's been stolen, broken, and hidden from our true selves.

I noticed within myself some deep disconnect and discontent, and in my previous work as a therapist, I saw this same theme play out over and again. It always seemed to lead me to a question: "Why do we live like we do?" That question has led me to understand just how much we have forgotten who we truly are, and how much there is to remember.

We must recognize what and *who* we have disconnected from, the lessons and deep knowing in our bodies, as well as our minds and spirits. The civil rights elders used the term "re-member" as a reimagining and reconnection in the context of bringing together a collective. This idea offers us a framework for how we might go about re-membering our own wildness and reconnecting with the natural world in our own returning. In becoming more connected with the natural world, we must open our hearts to listen to the collective voices around us: the voices of the trees, animals, rivers, seas, stones, and our human neighbors who are suffering.

In re-membering, we pull ourselves back together again.

What if we reconnect with our true origin and take note of what we might learn and synthesize? What if we awaken to the messages of the Earth and to our interconnectedness with all of creation? What if we engage in remembrance of where we come from, our ancestry, and our lineage spiritually and ecologically?

In July 2024 in North Carolina, I led a session on wilderness and worship where I walked everyone through an exercise designed to help participants remember their own experiences of the wilds of the world, and what those experiences taught them about Spirit and self. I asked everyone to silently remember a time when they sensed divine in the wilderness. I looked out across the people gathered and witnessed tears, soft crying, and smiling as everyone closed their eyes and recalled their experiences in the wild. The themes that emerged in this practice surprised me in how shared they were. Over and over, people felt the Divine in nature, the literal wilderness.

Spirit came through in impressions of goodness, nurturing, and inspiration.

There is power in remembering, and by remembering, we come home to ourselves, each other, and our more-than-human counterparts.

Remembering is also a reintroduction. Instead of going backward, we make a choice to move forward with this remembrance and allow it to change us.

Once you return to yourself and to who you were created to be, there is no going back to what my friend and author, the late Renée Altson, once called "paint-by-numbers spirituality."

Not only can you not return to what you previously considered as safe, you will no longer be able to see anything like it as safe again. You will recognize the inherent harm, danger, and seduction in the siren call of what you once knew.

Instead, you and I will hear the call of the oak tree who beckons us to sit in her shade and listen. We will find our safety and home in the rolling of the seasons, in the cry of the sandhill cranes flying overhead, in the rush of waves and babbling of brooks, and in the dim light of the stars in a darkened sky.

When I was a kid, my tiny elementary school's property was lined with trees. Next to the track which went around the school yard, there was a small stand of trees with an opening that created a half circle. My friends and I saw this place for what it was: magical. Several of us spent every recess playing underneath the trees, a perfect pocket of shade and mystery, like a natural fort we didn't even have to build. We would sit on the logs, pretend, and relish every minute.

In my own process of rewilding myself and remembering, I take walks in a pasture behind my house. I find myself crouching so I can walk the edges, the places where I can lose myself under the branches of the trees and where the deep green of chickweed creates a carpet of wonder. I listen for the sound of the majestic pear tree in the corner; when she says to come sit and rest, I do. I laugh with delight when my hat gets caught in the low hanging cedar and privet.

I know it might sound silly or maybe even absurd. But I am re-membering.

I am bringing back together the muscles of play with the bones of wonder. I am tuning the ears on my head as well as the ears of my heart to truly listen, and I am reconnecting with what had been drowned out by the pressures of adulthood and tools of distraction. The older and freer I get, the more I learn that absurd, seemingly foolish, and silly things hold the best stuff life has to offer, especially when it feels as though everything else is falling apart.

If you are also ready to remember, I invite you to think through the next exercise with me. Then we will explore together some other areas where we may have forgotten something we once knew so that we can reintegrate these messages and feelings into our being.

INVITATION:

Think back to when you were a child or adolescent. Consider what wild one might have offered you a shelter, a place to play, a delight or joy. Perhaps a tree or grove offered you a place to play. Perhaps you found delight in a squirrel, a dolphin leaping in the water, a bird in flight just overhead. Maybe you looked up at the stars and felt something you can't find words to describe.

Take in a deep breath, close your eyes, and imagine yourself with this wild place or wild being. Place yourself there and in that time of your life when you were younger.

What do you notice? What are you aware of in your body? What do you notice in your senses?

What inspiration, wisdom, or feelings do you receive from this sacred wild? What has this place or being impressed upon you?

How can you honor and remember this wild one in your life now?

CHAPTER 4
WILD RESILIENCE

WHAT IF REWILDING ourselves means remembering our capacity to come back? What if we were called back to remembering our strength? Our resilience?

In my previous role as a therapist and even now as a friend, I have often been astonished at the willingness of many people to give up when fighting for themselves. To be honest, I've noticed it in myself sometimes, too. I've wondered what has brought us to this point, and as I've walked through the forests and fields in the last couple of years, I've noticed my own sense of strength and perseverance rising within me. It called to mind my many walks and bike rides along forest paths when I was enduring the rigors of graduate school while also coming out of the closet one conversation at a time, how bolstered I felt with each trip to the woods. Then I realized it.

In losing touch with the wilderness, we have lost touch with our own natural resilience. A tendency has arisen to resign ourselves to our current status, our feelings of being stuck, with our words often giving voice to how we really feel. Phrases such as "I'm just not built like that" or "my brain doesn't work that way" or "this is just my life" tend to fill our vocabulary as we offer reasons and excuses for lack of movement, lack of connection, and lack of determination toward change. Unknowingly, we sit around in a new form of learned helplessness, captive in traps we've made for ourselves or been lured into by our cultures.

Instead of resilient, our social structure has made us stagnant and even stubborn when we face many challenges. In relationships of all kinds, we tend to choose easy paths instead of conversations or choices which might prove difficult. Sometimes we needlessly give up on healthy relationships and each other when the going gets tough. Some of us choose the escalators of relationship and family, career and vocation, and sometimes even our geographical location based on the lack of adversity or challenge, instead of what we most desire.

It's difficult to understand how people can live without technology and the comforts we have come to see as basic necessities. I tend to marvel at our ancestors' abilities to forge life in the wilderness, to grow their own food, and live through hardships and depressions. We forget that *we have that same capacity within us.*

Sometimes, I feel we have tamed our lives in every aspect, from food to sexuality to clothing to our ideas of Spirit and relationships. Life lived through screens and under fluorescent lighting has stolen our remembrance of what it means to die and be reborn, to fail and find the seeds we've borne through that experience to still be fertile. We've forgotten what it means to shrink under harsh conditions, only to bounce back again and again. Instead, failure and shrinking have become synonymous with endings and diversion from what we had hoped for.

But if we step outside, we see a different story unfold before us.

In what many would call "the *dead* of winter," I take a walk outside and notice what is *thriving*. I notice the stubbornness of purple deadnettle, small plants which have pushed through the dead grass only to face overnight temperatures below 10 degrees. Still, they remain green and vibrant; the wild flora thrive where the conventional have succumbed. Cocoons woven by small caterpillars which ravaged our young oak's leaves dangle from small branches in the gentle but cool winter sun. The small creatures remind me of the transformation possible during a season of dormancy and rest.

Meanwhile, the perennials of my garden, the walking onions, the irises, and the self-sowing zinnias and cilantro, rest beneath the earth, undergoing their own transformation and incubation, waiting for the moment they can be born anew. Unseen, but no less present, the microbes of the soil feed on the decaying remainder of last year's growth. Life doesn't just *find* a way, but rather *creates inroads and systems* to ensure its survival. And this happens again and again, like a song returning to its refrain.

I consistently experience awe when I consider how the Earth heals herself. I watch along the roadside where humans have cut down and uprooted trees, only to see months later that new wild trees have sprouted up in their place. Where soil has been left bare, wild plants abound to cover the precious earth. Where one of our old apple trees had been sick and dying, a sapling sprung up just before storm winds claimed the mother tree.

The wilderness teaches us that the power to carry on is within and among us all. Despite the harshness of winter, the power of storms, or the interference and destruction brought on by other people, not only can we survive, but *thrive*. What we need lives within our reach, within ourselves and our communities, and within the land in a symbiotic, reciprocal relationship. When we participate in creation with generativity, mutuality, and imagination, we practice our instinctual gifts.

I've been captivated by the idea of re-wilding and the tendency for nature to revive and heal when given the chance to, even after years of destruction and harm. A PBS docuseries called *Wild Hope* features stories like the 2011 undamming of the Elwha River in Washington State. This story shows us what's possible when we offer the chance for healing, wildness, and thriving. After the dam removal which had long been advocated for by the Lower Elwha Klallam people, the river began to carry silt again, thereby allowing steelhead trout and salmon to return to the waters and bring about the healing and restoration of plants, bears, birds, and native peoples who have long held the river as a sacred and life-giving entity. All have benefited from letting the river run free.

On a smaller scale, I notice the bees, butterflies, and birds returning in higher numbers to our yard as we let the clover, speedwell, and henbit live free and grow where they wish. The less we try to control our lawn, the more vibrant and full of life and color it becomes. At the same time, we watch as our neighbor sprays and mows his lawn incessantly in a battle against the natural, reaping results of brown patches where no amount of coaxing gets more grass to grow. The monocultural lawn stays devoid of birds, insects, and signs of wildness (or much life at all). While fireflies glow and butterflies flutter all over our area, none are across the street.

The consistent subduing of nature's resiliency disallows life to take root, all kinds of life. I can't help but wonder at how true this is within ourselves and in our communities and spiritual gatherings.

How often have we subdued our own resiliency by filling our minds with the distractions and the emotional overload of social media? By filling our bodies with highly processed food?

By filling our time with work and disconnection? By filling our spaces with items we don't need or enjoy? By obsessing with the rage and doom cycles?

Busyness, social media, rage addiction, the accumulation of stuff, and convenience food have become the pesticides and herbicides of our lives. (Not to mention many things that pass as food contain those things!) All of these disallow healing and rejuvenation to take root within ourselves.

I recognize another form of subduing our own resiliency when we take on messages we have heard or absorbed and believed them as truth about ourselves, the world, and the Divine. Too often, we believe in our unworthiness, our hangups, and our flaws more than we believe in our deservedness, our tenacity, and our strengths. Some of these messages originate from society, some from social media, some from our families, and some from our religious backgrounds.

No wonder we struggle to see the worthiness of each other or non-human beings when we obsess over our own shortcomings and downfalls. This leads us to feel even more disconnected, and leaves us feeling alone, unworthy, and incapable. But we are not bound to live this way.

I believe that by rewilding ourselves and re-membering, we can reclaim our resiliency in body, mind, and spirit. We can remember what it's like to forage for our food responsibly and in a way that helps the land instead of harming her. We can remember what it's like to put a seed in the ground and water it and watch a plant grow. We can remember what it means to sustain ourselves in the leanness of hardship and pain. We can remember how to nurture our selfhoods and our dreams into bloom and fruition. And not just individually. We can re-member our resilience in the strength of community, of coming together with other people and wild beings, and consciously returning to our place in the web of life.

INVITATION TO WILD RESILIENCE:

Take a walk outside, whether in your yard, a park or green space, or the woods. What life forms do you notice around you demonstrating their resilience? Perhaps a wild plant is growing through a sidewalk. Maybe you also see an area where trees have been removed before but are bouncing back. Is there a native plant thriving (or trying to thrive) where some cultivated varieties have perished?

Now, pause and take a breath to take it deeper. In what ways have you or your community gotten in the way of wild resilience? What habits of living have prevented regrowth and rewilding?

Turning inward, what lifestyle habits and internalized messages have stunted your own wild resilience?

What action steps are you willing to take to get out of the way of the wild resilience of the world?

(Examples might be leaving leaves on the ground, letting an area of your yard grow wild with native plants, stopping the use of pesticides and herbicides, etc.)

Choose one to begin acting on today as a first step.

What action steps are you willing to take to allow <u>your own</u> wild resilience to take root? (Examples might include a screen detox, changing an eating habit, choosing to exercise and build strength, etc.)

Choose one to begin acting on today, and take a first step.

CHAPTER 5
WILD ABUNDANCE

Among the harmful ideologies we adopt, one has proven especially difficult for me to navigate and work toward healing. It doesn't take long when listening to coaches or money experts to hear the phrase "scarcity mindset." For a long time, I grappled with embracing concepts of abundance because of the brand of spiritual trauma I had endured. In my church history, pastors demanding certain giving amounts, leadership blaming congregants' illnesses on a lack of faith, and what has often been labeled "the prosperity gospel," a name it and claim it approach to faith, warped my ideas of what abundance and scarcity actually mean. I couldn't even stomach the word *abundance* for many years.

But witnessing the role of plenty in nature finally allowed me to see the truth of what abundance is and is not. I finally experienced significant breakthroughs by this natural wondering, after years of working on cultivating a more helpful mindset. The Wild's natural state of reciprocity and nearby fields full of plants, birds, and insects offered me a wider and deeper view of what the world would be like without a lens of fear and lack.

I have found this abundance most among the blackberries. Where what many dismissively call "brambles" grow along the neglected fence lines, a summer treat and southern pastime beckons me to keep checking back. Though ignored, torn down, and disparaged by other people, I find an abundance of goodness to feed myself, my family, and friends from a plant that also provides food and shelter for the birds and rabbits.

Within the Sacred Wild, the message of abundance and generosity resounds with an infinite "yes!" The voice of wild abundance offers a strong counter to the messages of over-consumption and depletion that have misshaped the way we see the world. We tend to over-focus on what we do *not* have, what we desire, and what we can take for ourselves to our detriment as individuals, as communities, and as an injured planet.

I can't help but believe that much of our scarcity mindsets and fear of lack come from our separation from wildness and nature. We live as if we are outside of the web of life itself. I wonder sometimes at how much "not food" passes for food. How packaged, plastic, and synthetic items fill grocery aisles while we shop under fluorescent lighting. How often does a trip through a drive-thru or grabbing a delivery order at our doorway replace our connection and preparation with what we put into our mouths? How often are we too busy to care?

In my search for relief and healing from fibromyalgia, I sought help from an acupuncturist who also offered energy healing, Chinese medicine, and other Eastern health practices. As she placed the needles in specific areas, swung a pendulum over me, and used cupping to unlock my seized muscles, she talked to me about the importance of what I put into my body. In addition to the nutritional advice she gave me, one piece of wisdom stood out above the rest:

"Only eat food that has been prepared with love," she said quietly.

Surely, abundance and healing is rooted in the generous nature of love.

In the story of the Israelites journeying through the wilderness in Exodus, there is an account of mysterious bread appearing along with the morning dew, manna from heaven. Curiously, this manna comes with an instruction of trusting in abundance, to not take more than is needed and know it will come again. The Israelites are only allowed to store the bread for a day of rest; then they must return to the practice of daily gathering.

I see a similar theme as I watch animals eat the berries, nuts, and other wild foods available to them. They trust that there is enough for winter as they collect and eat, not chasing each other away. There is enough. I collect ripe blackberries that ramble across the fences and leave many for the birds, rabbits, and others to eat.

The tea I drink is ethically and sustainable sourced by a wild crafter who cares for the natural world with empathy and wonder. A young farmer at our local market shares with me how she wants to grow food *with* the earth instead of against her.

Abundance as well as understanding and trusting in this enough-ness leads to more sharing, more generativity, and more responsibility in how we forage and care for the life around us. The life of which we are also part.

And there is so much abundance around us! If not controlled, limited, and wounded, our yards can contain a multitude of wild foods and medicines, from dandelions and plantain to lamb's quarters and blackberries. I imagine this is what the visual of a field of possibility is all about: this beautiful regenerative full-of-life-and-goodness field. *This field* is abundant, both with life <u>and</u> all that life needs to continue.

How different this is from the limited time offers, the constant upgrades, the pressure to conform with the latest fashion, tech, and must-have-it-or-you-don't-fit-in items. All of these clog our social media, email inboxes, and shallow social interactions as they also fill our landfills with waste and our minds with scarcity.

Abundance does not equate to excess.

Late-stage capitalism isn't only bad for our planet. It's terrible for our minds and our hearts, limiting our belief and perception of true abundance.

Yet in the crook of the arm of Mother Earth, her song beckons us to remember what true abundance means, what we actually need and most deeply desire. Under the influence of her song, we begin to remember the truth and forget the lies we have been sold and have become addicted to. I can imagine her singing:

> *Lei lu, lei lu*
> *Remember my child, re-member*
> *Lei lu, lei lu*
> *In glowing my child, like embers*
>
> *The forests, the sea*
> *From mountains to bees*
> *All this and more*
> *Shall greet you*
>
> *When you, if you*
> *Remember my child, re-member*
> *See you, know you*
> *Are like them my child, re-member*

Forget now the haste
Let go of your waste
So much more to love
And be loved by

Lei lu, lei lu
Remember my child, re-member
Lei lu, lei lu
In glowing my child, like embers

After writing some of this book, I read the brilliant master-piece *Braiding Sweetgrass* by Robin Wall Kimmerer, and I found myself especially moved by the idea of reciprocal love with the land. Does the land love us back? Does the earth love us back? My heart pounded in my chest reading for her answer, the same answer I have come to know and appreciate: Yes. She loves us.

This love is abundant in the food we eat. In the shelter of trees. In rain that gives us water for life. In the funny way sand pipers run along the wave line. In the scent of pine, cedar, soil, and flowers. In the colors of strawberries, irises, limes, and pumpkins. In birdsong that has the power to lower our blood pressure, and the sound of rain on leaves and water lapping at a riverside. How she loves us!

If being loved by this world is not abundance, then abundance is either non-existent or utterly meaningless.

When we begin to reconstruct, reclaim, *and rewild* our ideas and beliefs about abundance and plenty, we begin to free ourselves from the empirical, colonized, and capitalist mindsets we inherited from our societies and begin to reclaim our birthright to inherited earth-wisdom. We start to notice the fill-ing-up and overflow we experience from a walk in the forest, a laugh with a friend, the sighting of a deer, the smell of rain, or a tomato from the garden.

Abundance then comes to be defined not in the next thing we can buy or gain, but in the living, breathing, relating, and knowing. Abundance, as we learn from the Sacred Wild, is found not in the future but in the present moment.

Perhaps, this is what Jesus, in his Aramaic language and culture, may have suggested when he spoke about having life and having it more abundantly. Maybe he was talking about the connection in this present moment to Divine Mystery. That when we are truly connected, that's when life is the most plentiful, the most full, the most overflowing.

The more I engage with this form of abundance, the more I experience this reality that being connected with nature and the Source in all things constitutes a truly abundant life. I recognize the exquisiteness of the call of the red-winged blackbird who visits each spring and summer. I drink in the colors and fragrances of spring as I breathe in and out. I relish the tastes of wood sorrel, blackberries, and pecans in my own backyard.

For those of us who have experienced financial insecurity or who have tended toward a more fear-based and lack-filled view of the world, this can be revolutionary. It's hard to have a lens of scarcity when we awaken to the fact we are surrounded by life giving life. It changes the way we seek pleasure when we slow down and enjoy what is natural and present. Our tendency to hoard shifts into a proclivity to share.

By leaning into the nature of plentitude, we open within ourselves more wells of receiving and more outflows of generosity and giving. We become more like the forest and the stream, full of life and thriving but also full of a cycle of giving and receiving that relishes in enough-ness. From this abundance, we abundantly love and give back to this beloved Earth.

Invitation to Awaken **to Wild Abundance:**

One of the most powerful things you can do to recognize wild abundance is to plant a seed and grow food. Another is to recognize the wild food and medicine abundant around us. Take a trip to your local library or research in your area what foods and medicines grow naturally in your location. What wild foods and medicines can be responsibly foraged where you are? If you are in a location where there are plant walks available, sign up for one.

In addition to these ideas, try this practice.

Go outside. This can be in your own yard or place of living, a local park, or a wilder area. If you live in a city, you might wish to get to a green space or park.

Once you are in your place, sit and open your senses. Notice through each sense the abundance and plentitude available. For example, through sight, you might notice the variety of colors, the depth of various hues and the play of light and shadow. Through hearing, you might take in the sounds of insects, wind rustling through plants, waves lapping at the shore or around stones, and birdsong. You might smell the scents of cedar or pine, earthiness or salt. Feel the many textures with your fingers and toes if possible. Notice any tastes in the air (or even among edible plants!). You are surrounded with abundance.

CHAPTER 6
COOPERATION AND INTERCONNECTION

Has there been a time when you felt lonely in the past couple of years?

Though our phones provide portals to connect with a multitude of people, the loneliness epidemic has continued to surge. Many of us crave connection beyond the increasingly artificial nature of social media and the shallowness and division that pervade our conversations and interactions. We desire embodied and in-person togetherness, especially now as we live increasingly online and isolated lives.

Talking with each other, much less working together, has become a rarity rather than the norm. Tech bros offer artificial intelligence as a possible solution to the lack of friendship, and that both disgusts and terrifies me. What is to become of friendship and authentic connection if we outsource it to tech?

Strict adherence to capitalism, limited ideas on work, and the never-ending pursuit of gaining more have not only stolen much of our time and energy, but also our ability to live in fruitful community. We have forgotten what it means to truly cooperate with one another, and instead rely on the myth of rugged individualism. We focus on our own ideas and distrust and endlessly deconstruct and criticize the ideas of others, especially the ones we find any fault or disagreement with.

We witness our isolation in our obsession with what we have been told to dream of: the big house, the right car, the right clothes. We feel it when it becomes harder and harder to achieve and maintain those things, and we feel squeezed by overcrowding. We hear it in the way we speak and continually prioritize "me" and "my" over "us" and "ours."

I fear for the society we have become, and for what it has cost us in our sharp disconnection from the cooperative ways of the wild.

We have been socialized, indoctrinated, and conditioned to accept individualism as the highest good and the strongest marker of health and adjustment. We question or ridicule people who admit dependency on others while we are socialized to both individualize *and* neglect our pain. In our age of artificial intimacy and pseudo-connection, we have learned not just to consume the things we are taught we should want and work to pay for, but we have also learned to consume and even monetize *moments*.

How often are our everyday sacred moments like having a cup of tea or coffee transmuted into pixelated images taken from the screens through which we've filtered most of our days? This then feeds into the pursuit of more consumption and more self-focus, often on social media feeds which we have looked to for feeding our sense of belonging and worthiness. Instead, we are fed modified versions of "truth," fluff, outrage, and advertising.

Meanwhile, I notice how much better the plants in my garden grow when I implement cooperation instead of isolation. I notice how little room there is in the woods for self-obsession, how doing so would interrupt the cycles of living.

We tend to believe that nature has our own human tendencies, that animals and plants compete for nutrients, water, and light. However, science is only beginning to tap into the depths of the wisdom known by Indigenous peoples for ages—that connection and cooperation are actually the norm in the natural world.

I watch the red-winged blackbird nest in the black cherry tree. He eats the cherries and spreads the seeds while the tree offers shelter for his family.

I notice the cyclical nature of air and water, and I find beauty and wonder in how so many trees store water which later benefits all around them when they release water through their root systems.

In the early hours of the morning, when the grey is giving way to dawn and the sun casts golden light across the green, cooperation can be felt as a presence in the air. In the dewy grass, the way the birds sing from the wild berry bushes, the chipmunks eating the seeds of the wildflowers, and the bees working the fresh clover blossoms, life is teeming with giving and receiving, taking and allowing for more life to come.

I sometimes wonder what would happen if we were to truly remember cooperative living as our innate mode of being. What if we awakened to the song and dance of life together and saw community and mutuality as the more natural choice?

Practically, I look beyond the beauty and ponder on the possibilities if we did this. What would it mean for housing affordability and sustainability if we found our way back to living in community? What would it mean for emissions and saving our planet if we shared more of our things like homes, cars, tools, camping gear, swimming pools, and gardens? What would it mean for our own health if we took the same amount of time spent on our screens and shared our time with each other and in the natural world instead? What more of a return would we receive if we "spent" our time and energy in ways that build connection, work toward common goals, and build a more sustainable way of life?

Our carefully curated online feeds and friend lists have created bubbles of isolation and disconnection that have furthered our heel digging and stubbornness toward in-group interactions only. While some things are not debatable, we've lost the ability and the desire to converse with people we may disagree with, and so many of us have become fearful and suspicious of neighbors, community members, and the people at the grocery store. I've been saddened at how many of my friends talk about not wanting to go outside of the larger city they've moved to or not wanting to visit their hometown in a more rural area because of how afraid they've become and how convinced they are of their protection of living in a city that's known to be more LGBTQ+ friendly. It particularly bothers me that this feeling persists, despite the numerous hate crimes and hate groups present in those larger cities.

Meanwhile, I attend the school events in a conservative, rural area for our kids with my wife, D, and I take note of the common ground we all have: love for our kids, and wanting to simply show up. I remember the way the birds occupy our feeders in the mornings, some on a feeder and some below and the fact that somehow they aren't fighting, but just being present together for the same reason. I imagine a reintegration of sorts, a way to just be together again, and a way to remember we are in so much of this—the polycrisis and the pressures and pleasures of every living moment—together.

If we remember.

And if we do the work.

That means we must also remember the ways we or our ancestors were not so cooperative and instead were violent, domineering, and divisive. We must remember and *do the work of reconciliation* for the atrocities that have been perpetuated. This means white people doing the work of antiracism and restoration and reparations for Black people, land being returned to Indigenous peoples, reconciliation and healing alongside queer people, dismantling ableism, true welcome and hospitality for immigrant people, and a healed relationship with the land and the more-than-human beings who share this Earth with us. Anything less than that is a "live, laugh, love" approach to cooperation and interconnection, and it's a fallacy to think that could ever be possible or desirable.

I believe that through this, we can do the work of becoming what the Rev. Dr. Martin Luther King Jr. called "the beloved community." And I believe this beloved community is an integral part of restoring our relationship with the earth.

Our earth-connection and cooperation with our planet can be healed through a systemic change in our lifestyles. Through engaging and living in community, we can turn our attention toward a reciprocal relationship with the land. Giving gifts of care and protection and attention to the fields, forests, and waters will yield more to share for all.

I had a phone call with my friend, Devi, an Earth lover who wrote a beautiful book chronicling stories on climate change. Devi is one of those people who walks through the world with wonder, attentiveness, and delight. She told me she had gone to visit a tree with a friend of hers who has had a hard time. These two friends sat under the shade of the tree, enjoyed the tree's presence, and drew and painted pictures of this tree all afternoon.

Coming back to writing now, I can't stop thinking about Devi's story. I keep thinking that this is the kind of sharing and mutuality I envision. What if we returned to relationship with the Earth for comfort, support, and even for relationships with other people?

Another memory comes to me. My family went to a local protest, and afterward, we were invited by our friend Aline to come back to her house. Our kids went outside to play, and the grownups sat in the yard under a grand maple tree. We tossed maple seeds in the air, chewed on wood sorrel, and relaxed into the Earth beneath our bodies. In the simplicity, the play, and the connection we were all soothed and rejuvenated.

In both my own experience and that of my friend Devi's, there lies an interweaving of something unspoken but just as present and tangible as the trees. Spirit, Divine Mystery.

Sacredness has been confused with ritual, specific behaviors, and even abstentions. But what if sacredness, instead, is attention to the here and now? What if sacredness exists *in the connection itself*? What if our interconnectedness with all things is actually where Spirit lives most actively?

Sometimes, spirituality is discussed in two dimensions, one upward focused on God or transcending while the other is focused on moving inward or downward into the soul. While both are important, I believe there is a *third* dimension, focused on the *interweaving* with each other, with nature, and all beings which can no longer be neglected. I believe this third dimension holds the key to much of our healing as a species and to the Earth. I also believe it is not enough to speak of this third dimension as simply connection with other humans. We must go further to mutuality, reciprocity, and interweaving.

The call to connection and cooperation requires us to see a deeper truth. Instead of trying to reach out to the margins and bringing people in, we need to move outward in order to truly connect with Spirit. While the church at large continually stresses evangelism, growth, and therefore its own importance, the Wild beckons us to come further up and further in so we can engage directly with the Divine in all.

When we connect and bring our awareness to our interconnection, we bring our attention to Spirit. This connection only deepens when we give our full attention. Too often, not only are our relationships fractured, so are our attention and focus.

We think of distraction in the sense that we can't focus on work, but this way of being has crept into our everyday living. Our constant distracted nature by tech, social media, and advertising robs us of deep connections and true presence when we are with other people and even when we are alone in nature. We spend increasing amounts of time on devices and screens, and struggle to keep them away when we are having a conversation or spending time with people we love. We've forgotten how to have real conversations, and a whole genera-tion of people who don't know how to talk to one another is choosing to speak through texting and messaging instead of talking, even when they are sitting next to each other.

If we are losing the ability to have analog conversations with the people we know, how much worse is it for talking with people who we don't know? How much more will it take to cultivate cooperation and community?

Unplugging and connecting with each other in real life, in our day to day, builds our muscles of remembering how connected we are and what it means to do life together. Being intentional to spend time with trees, barefoot on the grass, and near flowing water attunes us to listen again and reminds us of our mutuality and interwoven being.

I offer you an invitation now for your own remembering of interconnection. I want to give you an opportunity to move beyond the distractions and to truly attune yourself to the inter-connectivity. To do this, please be extra sure to not bring along any devices or at least have them turned off. Please do this with another person or group if at all possible. If not, then attune to other beings around you, and be sure to share this experience with someone afterward.

INVITATION:

Be somewhere where you can be connected directly with trees, water, or even grass. It's important for this practice that you be where you can directly touch and observe Wild connection. If this is not possible, houseplants and a bowl of water can be acceptable. For this practice, nature videos and photography are not a substitute.

In this space you have chosen, take a deep breath in. See the trees and plants near you. Breathe out. Continue to breathe in and out. Recognize that the breath you breathe in comes from the oxygen the plants near you are giving off. Recognize as you breathe out, that the plants are taking in the carbon dioxide exiting your lungs. Thank the plants near you. If you would like to touch them, ask permission first. Don't overthink, just listen with your heart to receive the response.

If you can be near water or have water with you, observe the flow of the water. Are plants near the water? Are they receiving life from the water? How might the plants and their root systems contribute to the life of the body of water? What animals are nearby and connected in this web of reciprocity? How are you also part of this web? How are you also water?

How might you interweave more with others, both human and more-than-human?

Carry this moment and reflection with you. Remember this when you breathe and when you drink. Please talk about this experience with someone, and thereby deepen and expand connection.

CHAPTER 7
THE ABSOLUTE NATURE OF EMPATHY

As PART of my own rewilding and journeying into the depths of an eco-spirituality, I have found my heart cracked wide open. This opening to me feels much like the way my heart stretched and opened when each of our children were born. In some mysterious way, even though I was already a deep feeler, everything became more amplified. More room was made for even more love, as well as more sorrow, joy, anger, and concern.

Now, as I find myself falling more in love with the Earth and rooted in connection with her, I feel a similar heart change. Not only do I feel deep empathy for people, I also experience deep empathy and love for animals, trees, stones, waters, mountains, and lands. I have become aware of the sacredness of every natural thing. And I carry much more grief for what we have lost and what we are losing.

It is especially hard for me to understand, holding a master's degree in counseling, having over a decade of experience as a therapist, and as someone who has a deep history with the Church, that empathy has lately become known as a sin or even toxic by some. Even as an undergraduate student in psychology classes, I knew what a true lack of empathy or disdain for empathy meant: a pretty serious personality disorder and a danger to others.

As a spiritual facilitator and guide, I see a deeper sickness and an even wider danger in this movement against our very nature. From a scientific perspective, we are wired to be empathic, to be able to understand and feel what another is feeling. Instead of sympathy, which is a removed state, empathy moves us closer in. And as researcher and author Brené Brown has said many times, it is hard to hate someone when we are closer to them. I would take this a step further and suggest: It's hard to exploit or disregard any being when we are living in relationship with them.

The movement against empathy continues to be championed by tech giants, Christian nationalists, and others who profit in money and power when we close off connection with our hearts. By moving most of our interactions from in-person to on-screen, we have already been removed further from each other. Our hijacked attention spans and image-occupied thoughts interfere with the possible depth of our conversations, and for many of us, we find ourselves in echo chambers. Facial expression and vocal tones provide immediate feedback, but the absence of them leaves us vulnerable to dehumanizing others. What might have been rare has become an everyday occurrence as more people spend more time interacting online rather than in-person.

A lack of closeness leads to a lack of empathy, and as we find ourselves caught in this vicious cycle, the antidote is to move in closer.

The original and most damaging social distancing was to get us to move most of our interaction and conversations to tech and online spaces. The distance and lack of empathy paves the way for business moguls to erect massive data centers which poison the land, steal and pollute the water, and displace humans and animals.

Distance and lack of empathy drive the industrial factory farms to destroy habitats, create health problems for our neighbors, and poison the waterways and lands. Not to mention the exploitation and abuse of hundreds of thousands of animals.

Moving in closer to truly hear and see what our neighbors, the land, waters, and more-than-human beings need in order to thrive would transform the way we live. If we know our neighbors, we will not want them to suffer. If we know the trees near us, we will not want them to die and be cut down. If we know the waters, we will want them to be clean and pure.

In rewilding ourselves, we must be in touch with our heart centers and recognize the absolute nature of empathy. Empathy is part of our biology, and denying empathy goes against our personhood, preventing us from being fully human and preventing us from being able to find solutions for the problems we face. Being able to recognize and understand not just emotion, but to understand someone's situation and perspective make up what person-centered psychologist Carl Rogers named "accurate empathy." When I was training as a therapist, I learned to understand this is the difference between knowing how someone feels and being able to sit with them where they are, and to better understand and have wisdom. It is only from a foundation of accurate empathy that we can create solutions and work for betterment.

From a perspective of accurate empathy, we can then know better what it means to truly love someone. We can better understand what is needed, what is desired, and what can help.

Loving is in our nature, and so is loving this world and the people and life which are in this world. In our deep disconnections, we have not only separated ourselves from the natural world, but also from the *nature of the world* and the nature of our own hearts.

Stretching our hearts again, like a muscle that has been unused, will come with some ache—only this time, in the form of grief.

We will awaken to the horrors of the many genocides and the level of destruction to all life. We will begin to see where we have been disconnected, complacent, and even complicit or culpable. We will bear witness to what we have lost and what's been given to us in return. We will see what's been left to us in the form of death, pollution, and legacies of harm.

But as we awaken to love and go through the grief instead of numbing it, we will recognize something else returning to us: the strength that comes from empathy and love.

As we return to deep love for this world and all within this world, we will find our strength to reclaim our place and to work for restoration. Instead of viewing Earth as some inanimate spaceship or temporary acting space, we will move more deeply into recognizing our oneness and restore our own relationship with the Earth.

The power of empathy and love, the power of our hearts, will connect us with the deep meaning and stamina we need in this long work ahead.

I TAKE a few minutes to scroll absentmindedly and witness person after person on my phone screen, cycling in the fear-anger-chaos-grief spiral. The panic and overwhelm becomes palpable, and I have to turn it off.

I go outside and walk around in my yard. I take in the way our blueberry bush has one more good harvest left. I decide to pick a few and leave the rest for wildlife.

I meander across the backyard and walk along the dead hedge I created and the native plants I have nurtured. I see several kinds of butterflies, native bees, and wasps on the flowers. I breathe a little easier. The garden teems with life and reminds me of what love looks like.

Our hearts take on what we immerse ourselves in. We cannot act in ways that are helpful and restorative if we are drowning in despair, but we also cannot act rightly if we numb ourselves, disconnect, or try to transcend reality.

As our hearts stretch and we begin to feel more sorrow, anger, concern, and grief, we will also know more joy. We will know more beauty and be better able to know the depths of peace. We will know the sweetness of what it is to love and be loved by our neighbors, by the waters, and by the land and all who inhabit nearby. We will know what it means to live in reciprocity.

Accurate empathy offers another benefit which we may not realize until we experience it: wonder and awe.

Sitting in space with clients and facilitating groups, I never cease to be amazed by the awe of truly seeing another. It is no small wonder to know someone, and we don't have to be a therapist to experience it. It happens in friendships when we go a little deeper. It happens in conversations with neighbors when we learn something we didn't know or when they make us smile unexpectedly. It happens when we walk into a forest or wade into a stream for the first time and take a deep breath as we witness the life there.

Understanding someone different than us does not happen through debate or arguing. It doesn't happen in vacuums or from reading an article. It happens in true relationship.

What would happen if we approached empathy and understanding from a perspective of wonder and awe? How might we better respect and listen with reverence? How would we differ in our approach to people? To animals? To the land and water?

In our everyday living, we make thousands of choices for who and what we allow in and who and what we attune ourselves to. As we move toward a more loving and rewilded way to live, may we remember to tune in to the power of our hearts and to the wisdom and nature of empathic relating.

INVITATION:

I invite you to practice stretching the muscle of your heart through engaging in accurate empathy. For this practice, select a wild being (more than human) to witness and reflect on. This could be a pet or animal in your care, a tree you can be near, a wild animal visiting your bird feeder or perched outside your window.

Observe this wild one. What do you see? What do you hear? What do you notice?

What do you feel in your heart toward this wild one?

Now imagine yourself in the place of this sacred wild being. What do you notice? What might you be concerned about? Habitat loss? Water pollution? Noise? What gets in the way of wild living?

Come back to yourself. Recognize what you feel within you. Grieve if you feel grief. But also connect with what you love about this wild one. What can you do for them? What can you do to help and become part of the solution for their life and wellbeing?

CHAPTER 8
WILD WONDER AND PLAY

When is the last time you played? How often do you take the time to imagine or play? What role does imagination have in your day-to-day living?

In our separation from the wilderness both outside and inside of us, we have also forgotten *who we used to be as children*. We have forgotten what it was like to depend on another, to be in our bodies in the here and now, to imagine and move freely and without concern for what others may think of us. We have forgotten what it is like to take in what is around us with wonder and playfulness.

I remember as a child having a sense of magic. I felt that my great-grandmother's hazelnut tree served as a portal to another world, a world of limbs reaching and stretching in all directions and leaves that could provide a perfect hide-away. I wondered at the fireflies glowing and dancing in the fields, the swirls of starlings that descended and covered the yard. I never failed to be mesmerized by the way the river sounded when it lapped against the shore, deep yet gentle and lulling.

As an adult, I have often had to *make* the time to stop and wonder. I remember the first time I looked up at the stars after what had been a very difficult first year of parenting. Between bedtime routines, battling a low milk supply, and a lack of sleep, I had forgotten to step outside and look up. I had forgotten what it felt like to look up into the night sky with awe.

When working in more traditional employment, my days were filled with conversations and computer-based work, all under artificial light. No amount of tree posters in my counseling offices could make up for the lack of windows or the distance from nature which I could only visit on lunch breaks or after work. How different this was from when I was a kid or even a teenager, when I had a little more freedom to be outside and more closeness with the natural world. And as I came home to spend time with our kids, I realized I had lost more than I thought.

Child development theorist Jean Piaget's famous quote "play is the work of children" stood out to me in my studies of psychology and counseling, but now I think of the phrase from a different perspective. In separating ourselves from our own wildness, we have forgotten how to play. I think, because of this, we have forgotten our truest work, the work we innately knew to do. Instead, we think of work as the way we make money. Though, under capitalism, much of that is actually more about making money for someone else.

D and I visited our kids' school for Field Day, a day of outdoor games and activities to foster teamwork and to celebrate the end of the school year with fun and physical challenges. After watching our daughter's class play dodgeball, we moved to the playground for their scheduled time there. We both laughed in wonder as we watched many of the kids run and begin to climb the playground equipment. One kid in particular swung from bar to bar, letting go and flying through the air on the monkey bars. Several kids climbed up the slide on the outside of its cover.

"I think when we stopped playing, we really lost that fearlessness," I said to D as we watched. "What if we didn't stop having recess at the end of elementary school? What would we have kept within ourselves?"

That risk taking and willingness to fall or fail empowered the kids to try the monkey bars, to try the cartwheels, and to make an attempt at sliding down the pole. I really do wonder how things would be different for us if we had somehow held onto that bravery. What if we had kept up with the swinging and climbing and maintained our upper body strength? What if we kept running and jumping and kept our quickness and agility? What if we maintained those muscles we used when we would play?

Have you noticed how much advice now tells us to sit and move like we did when we were kids? On the floor or ground, squatting, and bending and twisting our bodies to keep a range of motion. The point is to rebuild what we lost physically when we became too immersed in adulthood and stopped playing.

Our muscles of imagination may also be atrophied, but with some work of playfulness, we can begin to build them again, too.

When we visited friends in Vermont and New Hampshire, we went on many beautiful hikes that left us in awe. But along one trail in Vermont, our friend Devi showed us another wonder: Acorn caps make excellent whistles.

As we walked along the trail, we started collecting acorn caps of different sizes and tested them out to see how each sounded. Our kids stuffed their pockets with the ones they liked best, and even on the car ride home, the whistling continued on.

On another hike back home, our daughter was struggling

with feeling miserable in the heat and brush on a poorly maintained trail. So our friend, Vinay, got her to pretend to be a deer with him, leaping and laughing as she turned what seemed like a chore into play.

Play does not have to be elaborate. It can, and honestly should, be spontaneous, simple, and free of structure when possible. Somewhere along the way, we adults dropped free play and equated play with sports and games. Playing a game or a sport of course is a great way to play, but if we want to reclaim the wildness of play, we need to play in ways that are outside of the confines of rules, competition, and time. We need to be inside our bodies, our imaginations, and nature.

Our current unsustainable model of living—which many of us call late-stage-capitalism or industrial based society—does not allow for us to freely play as adults. We are glued to screens and desks, a clock checking our time, and constant demands for our attention. Scrolling, overwork, addictions, and binge-watching TV have taken over where play should reside.

I wonder how much freer we would feel if instead of streaming hours of television or movies, we laid on blankets to watch the night sky or clouds to see what shapes we can make out. I wonder how our minds and creativity would strengthen if we engaged with story and acted out in imaginative play and laughter. I wonder how our physical bodies would get more flexible and balanced and strong if we played in the natural world as we got older.

Over the past few years, I've made several friends who dare to play, and their play has become contagious in the best of ways. My friends Jess and Corey have encouraged me to bring more games into my life. My friend Naomi has taught me how to play with my voice and singing with others. My friend Steve has taught me how to play as a songwriter to create from joy. My friend Aline has shown me how to infuse playfulness in conversation and connection. My friends Michelle and Devi have awakened me to the playful nature of adventure and exploration.

Play can happen on a walk, while shopping for groceries, in talks with friends, and in other every-day moments. And the best way for us to learn this comes from those who know play best: children.

Because we've segregated children and adults throughout so much of our society, and because children are often seen as less-than or as people to control, we miss out on what we can learn from kids. Kids help us to remember who we are and who we were so we can re-member. They remind us what it means to imagine, to be light and unattached to time, to see the wonder and awe in everyday things. Kids pick up rocks and exclaim about how dear they are when we might think they look ordinary. Kids speak to trees and flowers and recognize special places made out of ditch banks and root networks. Kids intuitively know that animals have feelings and full lives of their own. I can't help but laugh along when the joy bubbles up in our kids as they delight in the Earth.

We were once kids, too.

As my mind wanders to spiritual community and how we gather, I can't help but wonder what would happen if kids were more included and allowed to speak. What would happen if we had more intergenerational times together? What would happen if we started getting more playful? When we teach children the names of plants and to pay attention, do we not also remember?

During our Wild Church gatherings, we allow kids to be "free range" and decide how much they want to participate or run around. I can't help but get misty eyed when kids share what they noticed in their own wander about in nature, or when a young child waves or speaks to a tree or shrub. This isn't waywardness or not knowing—it's a sacred intuition most of us have forgotten how to access. When we center children instead of dismissing them, we awaken our own child-likeness at any age. It's from this place of play and imagination that we can get a little wilder and a little freer, maybe even free and wild enough to invite others to play, too.

INVITATION:

It's time to play as a spiritual practice. Please invite someone along if at all possible! And if you know a kid or are a parent or grandparent, involve the kids so they can lead you.

Your task: Go outside and use your imagination. Create a kin-dom! Pretend that a tree is a magical house! Imagine walking through a threshold is a portal to a far away land! Talk with the more-than-humans and imagine their responses. Pretend to be an animal: move, howl, cackle. Pretend to be a tree: sway and rustle with the wind. Make believe!

These are just suggestions. Kids can help you be freer with your play. Do you feel silly? Good! Keep going.

CHAPTER 9
WILD WISDOM

PART of my journey into deeply remembering my sacred wild being began in an unexpected place, away from the wild. D and I were watching *Descendant,* a documentary about a ship used to transport enslaved people to Mobile, Alabama, known as The Clotilda, and the harmful legacies related to it. This film features so many important issues in institutional racism, the need for reparations, and the need for restorative justice. But it also provides a look into what else has been lost.

In one especially moving scene, a young man prays and speaks to his ancestors. I found myself deeply affected not just in the beauty of this connection he had, but in suddenly realizing how colonization and whiteness had stolen this connection for many of us in the west. Through tears, I recognized my own disconnection and lost relationship with my beloved great-grandmother and grandmother, both of whom I was close to when they were alive in Earth. Then, the grief of more hit.

Because of the institutions we have constructed as a western society, ruptures and fractures abound, including the separation from our own ancestors and the traditional wisdom we could have known. As I went back far enough, to my Celtic heritage, I recognized a close and deeply spiritual relationship to the land.

Part of re-membering for me is regaining this connection to elders. And not just in my family lineage or learning how my ancestors would have connected with Earth and Spirit. It also lives in intergenerational connections with people now.

For me, it is also in learning the deeply buried and unwritten histories of queer people in the South. It is in honoring, restoring, and recognition. It is in sorrow for what has been done in the past and in what has not been done.

It is in listening. And that includes listening to more-than-human elders, who have been here longer than we have.

When I stand beneath a tree who has seen several of my lifetimes, I cannot help but wonder what she has seen. I find myself drawn to sit and listen.

"Come, rest a while" one elder tree calls out with beds of chickweed and a log beneath her. I call her "Goody Alsop" like the beloved wise old teacher in the *All Souls* fiction series. I know she has deep wisdom and much to teach me, with her twisted branches, sprawling roots, and how she is surrounded by her younger ones.

She reminds me of my great-grandmother, Nanny Alloway. I once wrote a poem about her when I was sixteen. I called her a "strong oak of a woman."

Goody's branches weave and reach. Her roots do the same and cradle the earth.

The light through her somehow becomes more playful and enchanting.

She is steady.

She is constant.

She seems wry and witty somehow. Like the sparkle Nanny had in her blue eyes.

Like the rides in the car with my great-grandmother, there is a comfortable silence. It's a knowing and a holding all on its own. A woman who survived the 1918 flu epidemic, The Great Depression, World War II, and more—offering space to be. And so does this kindly old tree.

I wonder what this tree has seen. Who has been here?

But she is just focused on right now. And so I try to just be present, too.

I WONDER what it is that has led us to be so separate from the ones we most need: our elders. Why is it that we crave youthfulness and often discard the members of our society who know better? In our current times, a deep political divide between the old and the young furthers the chasm, but I can't help but wonder if our isolationism has fueled the deep misunderstanding and what we often call "ignorance." What if intergenerational relationships are the answer to bringing more understanding and acceptance? What if by better knowing younger folks, elders could better understand younger ones and what they care about and stand for? And what if by better knowing elders, younger ones could better understand where they come from, what has been lost in how we now live, and what could be re-found?

I recently saw a video of a senior man who showed up to protest against trans and nonbinary people at a local level in Wisconsin. Instead, he found himself listening to people who were willing to share their stories with him. Miraculously, he took his turn at the council podium to apologize and share how through this connection, he had a change of heart and mind.

Perhaps it is not so miraculous.

Perhaps it is the nature of heart connection.

In many cultures throughout the world, elders are cared for and part of the home. In the United States, though, we often discard our senior community members, even in instances when the care could be done at home and medical issues are not present.

In some places in the world, elder trees are revered and protected. In the U.S., old growth forests are harvested and turned into lumber.

When my wife and I got legally married in 2013, we took a trip to Lake Quinault in Washington State. Though it was during the time of a government shutdown and we couldn't visit Olympic National Park, we were able to walk the trails on the land belonging to the Quinault Indian Nation. On this side, we saw some of the largest, oldest, and most majestic trees we have ever seen. The world's largest Sitka spruce took our breath away, and we held our mouths open in awe as we walked among giants.

I grieve for the loss of forests like these. I grieve for the lack of old growth forests around me. I mourn that my children will not know some of the elder trees I once loved that have been cut down.

This discarding of the old has infiltrated our attitudes toward what is right, what is true, and what is best. We have discarded not just our elders, but the wisdom of our ancestors and traditions. We have lost the skills to grow, store, and make our own food. We have lost touch with understanding plants as not just food but medicine. We've lost the skills in repairing and making.

Even in my previous field of counseling, traditional and cultural understandings were often rejected in favor of what is called "evidence-based." Though, the "evidence" is often gained by studies which center cisgender heterosexual white populations among other strong limitations.

In many facets of our lives, we have rejected anything that is not rooted in the understandings that have been derived from colonization, and therefore white supremacy.

In my own efforts to restore this connection and re-member my own sacred wild wisdom and knowing, I find myself drawn to simplicity and returning to what I once knew. What my soul knows. What my cells know.

In May, I planted sweet corn in my garden. After wanting to for years, I had to finally get around to planting a three sisters section. Once my corn got high enough, I put my beans in the ground. When I visited my grandmother, I told her about what I had planted and how, and then she smiled and told me my grandfather used to do the same thing. That he always planted his beans with his corn instead of creating a trellis for them to climb.

I had no memory that he did this, but somehow the knowing was there inside me. My grandfather, who I did not see eye to eye with in so many things, yet still loved, somehow came through and connected in Silver Queen corn and the soil where we plant it. I can't help but wonder what other ancestral connections and wisdom I have been drawn to. Is this why I can't get enough of learning Celtic spiritual views and practices? Is this why I long to know more of where I come from? Which animals, trees, mountains, and bodies of water are imprinted in my DNA?

Where materialism has taken root, I open myself to intuition, to ancestral wisdom, to listening to the earth and more-than-human beings. It became loud enough in my heart that I had to leave behind my life as a therapist because of the profession's obsession with new science and a rejection of tradition, innate wisdom, and the mysterious. And because of the field's pathologizing of the human experience in times of crisis and upheaval, favoring a medical model over ancient knowing.

Perhaps the roots of rejection of the old are fear of death, fear of irrelevance, fear of being forgotten. And instead of keeping the memory of others alive, continuing a legacy, and remembering and honoring elders, we discard them and thereby perpetuate what we are most afraid of, continuing the vicious cycle.

Perhaps we are afraid of grieving.

And yet we must grieve. So much has been lost to us. So much has been lost to our children. So much has been lost to the descendants we may never know. So much is actively being lost.

One day, we too will be ancestors. One day, we too will hope to be remembered, honored, and that our legacies of goodness might continue.

While going through the Wild Church Leadership Course, I was introduced to *The Lost Words*, a beautiful project of poems and songs inspired by a tragic shift in language, marked by the omissions and edits in the Oxford Junior Dictionary. Instead of preserving nature-based words like "acorn," "dandelion," and "heron," those and many other words of our wild world have been replaced with the words of technology such as "blog" and "broadband."

When our course facilitator, Valerie, started sharing the story behind this, I suddenly started to weep. Even writing this now, I feel the mourning in the tightness of my throat and in the tears that fill my eyes. I immediately thought of my own children and the legacy, wisdom, and deep knowing I hope for them. I long for them to know the sound of cicadas, the call of wrens, and the names of the tiny wonders at our feet. I want them to know the softness and resilience of moss and the potential of a mighty oak found in a tiny acorn.

In order for our children (and all children in the next generation) to carry on the wisdom, we must reconnect with the deep wisdom ourselves. We must rediscover the simplicity, the connection, and the rhythms of sacred wild being. We must reclaim the things we *should* know. Perhaps we weren't even taught them, but we can find ways to learn through books, workshops, and most importantly, by spending time with those who carry this knowledge.

Part of rewilding ourselves means returning to traditional and ancestral wisdoms. While I am grateful for modern medicine, I also have found great healing and value in herbal interventions, acupuncture, massage, and other healing arts aligned with nature. I have started doing my best to garden and align with the cycle of the moon, like my ancestors of Appalachia did.

I invite you now to take time to reflect on how you might connect with the wisdom you may have forgotten or even rejected. The following invitation encourages you to connect deeply with the wilder ways to live so that you may pass them on. It's up to you to continue in this work and to share it as part of your own, and our collective, legacy.

INVITATION:

In this practice, I invite you to connect with your elders and ancestors.

Often, we only think of our ancestors as those who may be in our family trees or lineages. Some of us have only partial histories available to us. Some of us were adopted into family lines. Some of us have elders important to us who are outside of family histories. Some of us have chosen families.

But all of us come from the Earth. All of us share elders in the form of trees, stones, mountains, rivers, shorelines, mammals, birds, and insects who were here before humanity.

Consider which of these elders is calling to you. In an outside place, look around you and observe who here is your elder. Who here has wisdom of being alive in Earth before you were born?

What does it feel like to be in the presence of an elder one?

What do you notice within you when you look at this elder?

How do you feel in your body when you consider the wisdom and knowledge this being has?

What lessons might they have?

How might you thank them and carry them with you in remembrance and honor?

CHAPTER 10
RECONNECTION

RECONNECT WITH SELF

My work is rooted in my deep belief that we hold the answers and empowerment for change within ourselves, even when we don't recognize that. Time after time, I have journeyed with people I've worked with as they've tapped into reclaiming their own knowing and wisdom, as well as their personal power. But in order to get to that place of reclaiming, the work required digging deep through the years of mud and overgrowth down to the bedrock of connection with self.

For many of us, remembering includes a co-requisite of re-membering our true selves. Layers of messaging from early childhood on often misshape and distort our self-view and create our individual personas, or the masks we wear and too often mistake for our true identity.

If you are expecting my next line to be about "identity in Christ," I'm either going to deeply disappoint you or deeply affirm you in telling you that I believe this is yet another layer placed upon us which has created more disconnect. For those of us in the LGBTQIA+ community, this insistence has been welded against us like a weapon, urging us to "deny ourselves" and exchange our divinely created way of being for compliance and death of our truest selves. This teaching often comes on the tails of what is known as penal substitution atonement theology, which many of us were taught to equate with the only valid view of Jesus, his death, and resurrection. In this idea, a wrathful God had to be appeased with blood sacrifice, an understanding of Spirit as a distant, vengeful, and temperamental deity.

I deeply believe that Jesus also would offer us a gentle (or perhaps not so gentle) reframe of this way of thinking about identity. When we dive into the teachings of Jesus, especially within the context and richness of the Aramaic language and worldview, the message of all of us being part of Sacred Unity rings throughout. Our belovedness and worthiness comes not from saying a certain prayer or confession. Rather, our truest selfhood comes from our being.

The sacred unity, unifying and loving, ever-becoming, ever-expanding essence offers us a glimpse of what we might embrace within ourselves and each other.

How differently might we live if we truly believe in something like the Imago Dei, the idea of our being created in and continuing to embody the image of Divine?

How would we treat our bodies and remember the goodness of our physical selves?

How would we better trust our guts, our spirits, and our minds?

How differently would we understand our relationship with the world?

Somewhere along the way, many of us traded in our divine image for the lie we are inherently broken, damaged, and evil. We bought into a traditional creation and original sin narrative which was created in the midst of suffering as if it were the literal truth. This further severed our selves from the natural world and from Source. Separateness began to take precedence over togetherness. Individualism rooted where cooperation and interdependence once thrived much in the way kudzu, an invasive vining plant, has overtaken roadsides and parts of forests. Now the kudzu-like vines of ego, hyper-individualism, and sectarianism intersect in an overgrowth which must be cut back and cleaned off to reveal the bedrock of the mountain of who we truly are.

We do not find who we are. We do not only become who we are. Rather, we become and grow into our truest selves in the context of relationships. For us to find our truest selves, we must also restore our relationship with the natural world.

Reconnect with Nature

In July 2024, D and I did something I'd wanted to do for years—go to Wild Goose Festival—a music, arts, and justice festival rooted in inclusion and progressive Christianity and spirituality. While the connection and the beauty of so much incredible music, art, and conversation surpassed my expectations and deeply touched me, one element truly surprised me in how much it affected me. Living outside for a few days in the summer in Eastern North Carolina.

With just a tent between us and the night, we slept beneath a tree and spent our days on grass and in natural light. Life outside became a norm much quicker than I anticipated, despite the hot and humid weather. On the hottest day, a bandanna soaked in iced water cooled our necks. We gravitated toward the shadiest spots and ate cold watermelon to help us stay hydrated along with copious amounts of water, some salty snacks, and coconut water.

During nearly every session, a breeze would come across those of us there, gently rustling the tent fabric and giving voice to the leaves as they sang in the trees. I became acutely aware of the songs of birds and insects, and the many shades of green and brown and present all around me. I couldn't help but feel the presence of Spirit in the wind. At night, as we made our way back to our tent or visited the port-o-potty in the middle of the night, I noticed Scorpio and Ursa Major in the sky, like old friends I hadn't seen in a while stopping by for a visit to see how I've been.

I recognized my own tendencies to shelter inside during the summertime. And while the heat and humidity are often unbearable and even worse during perimenopause, I realized that I have unnecessarily kept myself away from the heat. I realized how much I have missed by trading my own wilds for comfort to paraphrase a Rising Appalachia song.

From walking a prayer labyrinth, to playing in a drum circle, to dancing and howling, to singing and holding deep conversation, nature and the softness of the outdoors held all of my experiences and held me as I branched out and made new connections. We were held as we all engaged in community and presence with each other and the Earth.

As D and I climbed in our van to drive back home, I found myself adjusting the thermostat higher than I normally would, the air conditioning feeling too low and somewhat shocking. We talked about how meaningful the overall experience had been for both of us, and how hard it was to leave what felt not so much like a wonderland as a return to how it should be. I cried from a place of gratitude but also grief and a bittersweetness. We would be returning home and reuniting with our kids, pets, and a real bed but at the cost leaving behind the kinship and the celebration of diversity. At some point, I also realized my sadness of leaving behind so much closeness to the Earth and time spent outside.

After returning home, I struggled to adjust and find ways to live outside more. I've taken my laptop and notebooks outside to work in the mornings before the heat becomes dangerous as we've been under heat warnings galore over the summers. I try to take as many walking breaks outside as I can.

Yet, I've noticed that even on the days when I'm forced inside due to excessive heat or storms, when I make time to connect by being present outdoors, something shifts inside of me.

When I replace artificial light with natural light, I see more clearly, both with my eyes and with my heart and mind. When I open my ears to the mockingbirds, wrens, and crows, the rustling of plants, and the buzzing of insects, I become more aware of the isolation of insulation.

I wonder sometimes about how I can reconnect with my wildness more, how I can bring more connection to nature. Over and over, advice in books and online suggests that we bring nature inside: plants, leaves, stones, and wood. As someone who favors a rustic style of décor, I of course am more than willing to do this! I also do believe this can help, especially if we engage with more than one sense. But what I am finding is that perhaps the outdoor companies have the best solution and often say it best, simply "get outside."

We all have a tendency to tell ourselves myths. As a writer, I often tell myself I can't write unless I have at least one hour. This is despite the fact that I have sometimes written my most beautiful prose while walking the dog for ten minutes. I also have been guilty of talking myself out of going outside at all if I can't stay out for a long period of time or that it's only going to be helpful if I am in a more remote area or on a trail where I can feel immersed in the forest.

While the smell of pine needles and earth and the rhythms of trail walking do offer a more potent and lasting remedy, I am discovering that even a 10-20 minute walk or sit outside on the grass or near a tree offers me a chance to remember who I am and to reconnect with the natural world. Maybe it's not just the long times we need in nature, but those intermittent times that enact our muscle memory of our own wildness and belonging.

INVITATION:

In this practice, we will theoretically feed two birds with one hand (this saying is a more beautiful alternative). This particular practice will get you outside, and will allow you to practice getting down to the heart of your true self. This might take some scheduling and planning, and it's best done with others. It's also best done if you have a little knowledge first.

Invasive Species Management: Just like we talked about with invasive kudzu, there are many invasive species that crowd out native plants crucial for wildlife. I invite you to take part in removing them from landscapes so that native plants can thrive. What is most needed will depend on where you live geographically. This is *not* weed removal. What many of us refer to as weeds are actually crucial native species for our local ecosystems, and this is not a "go in and take them all" kind of task (and you know by now, it's certainly not about using any chemicals). This is about management, not eradication.

The best way to get it right is to partner with a park, local sustainable farm, or outdoor or plant conservation organization that can help guide you on recognizing and correctly removing a species. As an example: Kudzu overtakes even trees. It's become a menace for many species, but it's easy to recognize for removal. The Nature Conservancy is a good resource for learning more.

I know this asks a lot of you. I mentioned rolling your sleeves up, and this practice really requires that, and a good pair of gloves. If you are not physically able to remove invasive species, you might do what you can, help spread the word, and perhaps you can also watch some of the process. What you learn, you can take home and continue to practice.

While you are removing the invasive species or watching, identify and reflect on what has taken over to obscure your own true self. What is revealed when you remove what does not belong? What had you forgotten or ignored that was there? How might you reconnect with these aspects of your true self?

CHAPTER II
SPIRITUAL PROBLEMS

For many of us who have woundedness and trauma in our spiritual and religious experiences, reconnecting with Spirit often feels dangerous and maybe even dogmatic or prescriptive. I once received an angry response on social media when I described the need for being in touch with our spirits and went on to define spirituality in the broadest of terms: "the things that make life juicy and beautiful and worth living." Several strangers accused me of being unempathic, shaming, and most intriguing to me, said I was telling people they have to be spiritual.

I don't believe that we have to be spiritual. Rather, I believe that we all *are spiritual beings.* Just as we suffer from a great disconnection from nature and from each other and from our bodies, many of us suffer from a great disconnection from Spirit, both our own and the Source/Oneness that we are all part of.

From the research of British journalist Johann Hari in his exploration of depression in *Lost Connections* to the "Blue

Zones" work of longevity researcher Dan Buettner, we witness time and again a scientific and data backed acknowledgment of what ancient wisdom has taught us across a variety of traditions. The soul matters, and spirituality offers improvements to our health and wellbeing.

In my work as a therapist, I learned that when we internalize anger and refuse to move forward and onward, we diminish ourselves further and further. While what has happened to us is not our responsibility, we do have the *opportunity* to offer ourselves healing and support by re-engaging and reconnecting with our spirits. For those of us with spiritual trauma, we may need therapy, coaching, or other healing work with an experienced practitioner to help us journey through that process. This might also require practicing self-compassion like the incredible work of self-compassion pioneer Dr. Kristin Neff teaches us to do. We can further our healing work through practicing forgiving ourselves, another person, a community— whatever and whomever we need to forgive for our own healing.

As D learned in a workshop she attended on forgiveness: Forgiving is not for the offender. It's for the person who has been harmed. It's a release that means we don't have to dwell on this anymore, and in choosing to not dwell on it, we improve our immune function, our mental health, and allow ourselves to move forward. To be honest, it's still hard for me sometimes to remember that.

Healing is never a one-size-fits-all approach. We all need something different. With an attitude of openness, loving ourselves, including our spirits, positions us to be able to receive healing and take an active role in our own betterment. It also helps us address the deep spiritual problems in our world that contribute to the challenges we collectively face as a planet.

Deeply spiritual problems call for deeply spiritual solutions.

We currently live in an age where much of the Western church has wed itself to nationalism, crass and violent behavior, racism, xenophobia and queerphobia, and a host of other prejudices. The institution has exalted lies over truth and rulership over justice and mercy.

This is nothing new. We can look at the history of the church and remember the ways the church has wed itself to empire before, all the way back to many male leaders at the helm bowing to the Roman government that forced both citizens and the church to fall under the rule. We still reap the consequences of what they sowed thousands of years ago.

We can look at the religious leaders in the time of Jesus, the Pharisees and Sadducees who aligned with the empire to kill Jesus and their attempts to kill his message and teachings, as well as torture and kill his followers. In some ways, it seems they succeeded. The message of Jesus of Nazareth has been so warped, mistranslated, and misused, it is beyond recognition from the Aramaic words Jesus spoke. Instead of following in the way of love, much of the church became singularly focused on hero worship and rule-making.

When we look closely, we see the true nature of what we face. *Empire is the ancient enemy of Spirit.*

Spirit wishes to serve. To connect. To create and thrive with generosity and unboundedness.

Empire seeks to control. To isolate. To tear down, profit, and hoard with scarcity.

In the desire for more power, the evangelical religious right has grown Christian nationalism into a machine not unlike the logging equipment that tore down the forest near our children's school in order to make room for expensive housing.

The relentless greed of those in power finds its fuel in the current pressures to acquire as much money and assets as possible, just to buy even more. Our personal ideas of success have become warped. Even within progressive expressions of the church, this constant striving for an elusive more drives decision making and often requires the sacrifice of what matters most.

Perhaps these spiritual problems began with a seed, in the deep disconnection with our own spirits, with Earth and the wondrous beings we fail to even notice. It rooted into our hearts with deep failures, starting with our own cosmologies and origin stories which wove the threads of false narratives concerning our role on this planet. For some of us, this even went to the extent of conceptualizing our own planet as Godless and in need of saving. Nothing could be further from the truth. For still others, the Eden story reinforces false notions of dominance, shame, or both.

Because of the decisions of men leading the church and their desire to exert control, many of us were taught to only consider the Bible as scripture and sacred. But in reality, an ancient sacred text that predates the Bible and was long revered as the original scripture was then discarded. That sacred text is the Earth herself. This decision further separated us from Earth and together with the traditional Biblical creation story caused us to miss the importance of our planet and how we are part of her.

In responding to the constellation of problems resulting from our disconnection, we must return to this original sacred text so we can better understand where we've been led astray and the many spiritual disparities that have followed.

We must also understand how worship of the written word and its sovereignty have been wielded as weapons of oppression, colonization, and white supremacy. Creeds, theological pontifications, and the like have replaced direct knowing of the Divine through Earth connection. We have forgotten to look to the stars, to place our hands on a tree, to put our bodies in water and then to listen and know.

We suffer from a disparity of deep knowledge and wisdom.

We suffer the disparity of thinking our bodies are separate from our spirits, not good, and merely vessels.

We suffer from a disparity of viewing Earth in much the same way we view our bodies: temporary, not good, not worthy, and separate.

If we are to reclaim our deep wisdom and knowledge, if we are to reclaim the goodness and connection with our bodies and the Earth, then we must heal and restore our relationship.

Growing up in Southern Christian fundamentalism, I understood spiritual healing to be more about God than me. I understood that I was flawed and broken and weak, but that Jesus was strong and perfect enough to heal me. Healing, I thought, was somewhat passive and more about allowing. My role was to purify myself through repentance, self-flagellation and self-denial, and abstinence from sinful behaviors and thoughts. Jesus would do the rest for my soul.

Instead of healing from my sexuality, because that's the one area I couldn't perfect, I developed a deep fear, disgust, and distrust of myself. Instead of healing, I got sicker. And this sickness even manifested itself physically as my body kept the score of every time I was taught that who I am is sinful or evil. Instead of healing my heart and moving closer to the Divine, I felt blocked and cast aside.

I'm not the only one. And it doesn't take being in the queer community to experience this flavor of shaming and ostracizing. What I call *covert spiritual trauma* is rampant toward all kinds of people as we were taught to view ourselves and even all people through doctrines of original sin, "worm theology" that states we are unworthy and lowly creatures, and other harmful teachings.

This is not spiritual healing.

True spiritual healing reconnects us to our truest selves.

True spiritual healing invites *all* of who we are, affirms the goodness of our whole selves, and requires us to take action that builds and creates.

We build connection. With our spirits, bodies, and minds. We create and re-establish relationship with our selves, with other people, with the Earth, with Source. We restore our kinships and our souls.

In mid August, in the golden light shortly after sunrise, I find myself drawn outside. What calls me there this particular morning is not the birdsong or the warmth of the sun. The morning dew calls to me, invites me to put my feet in the grass. The urge strong and my heart listening and eager, I step barefoot into the green of my front yard, feeling somewhat vulnerable to the traffic going by in the weekday morning rush.

The moment my feet meet the soft and damp ground, I find a new footing and way to stand. I take a few steps toward a young dogwood tree we planted, mesmerized by the glistening drops on the edges of leaves. But then a shaft of sunlight draws me further out from the front porch, more visible to the road and passersby, but irresistible. The soles of my feet take in the warmth of where the sun has touched the grass, and I look down to witness dew drops suspended and shimmering on my feet.

Somehow, my eyes close and fill with tears. I notice the cicadas' song, the lawn mower next door, the birds chirping, and the cars going by, all present and connected. I open my eyes again to that glorious light, caught up in the dew drops on my feet like magic.

My mind wanders to Gideon, placing out a fleece as a test, asking for the dew to only land on the fleece, asking for the fleece to remain dry from the dew, all in a question to God. I find myself not wanting to say the word "God," feeling that the word doesn't do justice to what I just witnessed, finding that the harm done and the moment we are in just doesn't make sense with all the baggage and wrongness that word and concept carries. But I find myself in a testing of Spirit anyway.

My feet are wet and glistening, and I close my eyes again and hope we are delivered from empire. I offer what to the poet Mary Oliver might be a prayer as I long for our own recovery and restoration.

By the time I reach my door, the dew still clings to the tops of my feet like a remnant of where I've been, staying with me wherever I go. Perhaps the drops are there to remind me to stay grounded in interconnection. Perhaps they remind me to step into both light and shadow. Perhaps they call me to remember my kinship and role in delivering myself and the precious ground from empire.

This is what it means to restore my soul. This is what it means to be embodied as my full self, present and alive in the Earth. This is what it means to embrace the kinship-of-all-things.

No hymn or modern worship song can take us there. No sermon or treatise on a theological concept or view.

Only bare feet, an open heart, a sense of wonder, and presence with our senses. It is only then that we may know how to be idle and blessed and heal the deep spiritual problems we face. This is what it means for empire to crumble and rewilding to root within.

INVITATION:

In some cultures, including some Celtic traditions, bathing in morning dew was an important spiritual practice marking specific holidays and turns in the wheel of the year.

I invite you to engage in this dew centered practice** with other people if you can, but alone works, too. I invite you to approach this dew practice as a rooting of yourself within the Sacred Wild.

Go outside in the morning light. If you can be outside at the golden hours, that is even better.

Notice where the dew (or frost) is clinging. Notice how a single dew drop can be suspended on a leaf, a stem, moss, or a blade of grass. What colors reflect back to you from the glistening drops?

Notice how the light plays in a single drop as well as in the collective drops of dew.

If you can walk barefoot on the grass, do. If you can't, feel the dew with your hands. Notice how the drops of dew feel on your skin, and observe them with your eyes. How do they feel or look suspended on your feet or hands?

Wash your feet or hands with the morning dew by rubbing a few drops on your skin. As you feel the dew, you might think of the renewal offered to you by this gift. You might ponder how this renewal offers you a fresh beginning and consider what you would like to begin or begin again in your relationship to the Earth.

Give thanks to the dew and to the Earth for the beauty and gift. It might be a "thank you" or a song or poem or watering a plant, feeding the birds, or caretaking in another form.

**If you are reading this at a time of year when it's too cold or dew is not available, or if needed for any other reason, you have two options for alternatives. 1: Collect dew in a cloth by laying it outside on the ground overnight. Wring out the cloth

into a bowl or cup. 2. Collect rain water or snow/ice/frost (which will need to sit and melt). Be inside in an area with natural light if at all possible.

Proceed with the practice by placing drops of dew, rain, melted snow or ice on your feet, hands, arms, etc.

CHAPTER 12
THE STORY OF SACRED EARTH

For all of my life up to this point, I have studied the Bible and what it has to say about the Divine, the world, about me, about other people, and about the meaning of it all.

I started very early in life with singing songs and listening to the big stories from the Bible while Sunday school teachers used flannel graphs or object lessons to prop up their points. I won Bible trivia every time we played in children's church or at home. By the time I was a teenager, I was leading my own Bible study at my high school, planning sermons I couldn't give (because I was a girl in a denomination that did not allow it), and even using my knowledge of the Bible for apologetics (an evangelical form of arguing and persuading).

In adulthood, I have taken many college-level classes on scripture and theology, and I've done deep dives into particular books, followed the lectionary calendar, and prepared and delivered sermons. I have read the Bible all the way through several times; plus I've read many commentaries, devotionals, and spiritual books which all use scriptures to make their points.

But I have to tell you, even if I kept this up, I know deep in my bones and in my heart that I will not know more of the Divine, or of this Earth or of myself and other people. Maybe, most importantly, I certainly would fail to understand more about the meaning of it all.

Instead, I want to spend the rest of my life seeking, studying, and divining through nature, relationships, and firsthand encounters that are too mysterious, precious, and life-altering to even begin to be translated into the written word.

I long to spend the rest of my life knowing and believing and trusting my body, my senses, and my heart as well as the water, the air, the fire, and the earth. I want to lean into wisdom and ancestral knowledge rather than scholarship or research.

In studying a more Celtic view, I learned of the ancient tradition of seeing the Earth as sacred text. It is actually in the more modern versions of Christianity that seeing everything through a lens of "scripture only" has become the norm. Of course, this view transpired at the same time the religion of Christianity became entangled with empire.

In Wild Church, we often talk about restoring the sacred conversation, meaning restoring the connection we have with the earth and with each other.

When I listen to the green ash tree in my yard and hear the wind rustling through her leaves, I open myself to understand something new. When I watch the way the fire dances on the logs and feel the warmth moving outward, I can learn something about Divine Mystery that I cannot find anywhere else. In the space of the in-betweenness of my friends and in our collective voices rising together in song, I hear another story emerge about meaning and love and mystery.

In the past couple of years, I have awoken to understanding Spirit and connecting with Divine Mystery through the natural world. Now I have recognized that each day and each encounter offers me a new perspective. Instead of analyzing or exegesis or even deconstructing, I have found that in the living and being, there is an opportunity to be in active participation. Instead of living in my head, I am leaning into living in my body and into my wholeness and relationships.

When I directly experience Source in nature, in some ways it reminds me of my roots in Pentecostalism. Though I do not ascribe to that system of beliefs any longer, the idea of direct, uncontrolled, and mysterious encounters with Spirit does resonate with me—perhaps more now than ever.

Somehow, we have forgotten how to have a direct connection and direct relationship with other people, and it's even worse when it comes to relationship with the Earth and all beings. We tend to have our phones ready and immediately pull them out when we see something in the natural world that captivates us. Instead of connecting and honoring and being captured by the moment, we want to capture and share it in the post so *we* can capture attention.

Natural encounters have become a commodity in our attention-based economy. So then, radical resistance and repair of that relationship looks like engaging with nature in the least showy ways possible. It looks like tending to a garden and paying attention to what the plants need. It looks like walking through a forest without the premise of exercise or summit or waterfall pictures. It requires us to be both fully present and fully open to connection that is rooted in reciprocity. It looks like creating new and restorative stories through a process called *re-storying*.

Because so much of our relationship has been founded on stories that are not so helpful, we need to go back and see what we have missed, what we have needlessly carried, and what we have neglected or dismissed on purpose. When I first read Robin Wall Kimmerer's *Braiding Sweetgrass*, I found myself so captivated by the story of Sky Woman that I read it over and over before moving on to the rest of the first chapter. In this Haudenosaunee creation narrative, a woman plays an integral role along with animals in the creation of the world.

I grieved over the fact that the story I was taught about creation was so damaging and even traumatic to me as a woman. I mourned, too, that the story I was taught seemed so limited and so human-centric. Not only was the Genesis story written in a way that centered humans, but the people who taught it to me also taught each day of creation as if it were building a foundation for human existence and in order to serve men. (And I do mean men specifically.)

Embedded in the story I was sold, and that I bought into for far too long, lay more lies about myself. It encouraged me to believe that my body was bad and that I had been born sinful and not good. The old story asked me to give up my own inner voice of wisdom and instead believe that my mind was filled with trickery and the potential for deceit. As a gay woman, the story informed me that I was made to please and serve men and the only natural way to love was to deny my true self and the true love I was ready to share.

The old story taught me that plants, animals, water, and fire were created for humans to use as we please. In this view, animals and plants, and certainly rocks and water had no sentience. Human supremacy embedded itself from the get-go, and this origin story continued to be referenced in other stories which drove the point home even more.

But when I walk among the trees and listen to the birdsong emerging from the branches, I hear a new story emerging. Or more accurately, I hear a more ancient and truer story. It's the story I was meant to hear. The story that was censured and disparaged to favor empire and dominion.

In the true story, I recognize I am a child of the Earth. In the ancient knowing, I can find my belonging in a great web of interconnection and life. I recognize my place as an animal and can realize the elements within my make-up. Earth minerals add strength and stability in my bones. Water courses through my blood and my tears, my sweat, and through my brain as thoughts weave their way through. Fire dances in my belly, converting food to energy. Air fills my lungs and sends oxygen about, animating me. When I tune in to this story, I know that I am connected to all things.

For too long, *both* materialism and religious doctrines have led us to seek knowing only from external sources like written words, scriptures, scientific studies, data, observation, and experts. We are in a critical moment when we need to return to *inner knowing* and *inner wisdom*. Within our bodies, our intuition helps us to filter what stories are true and which ones we feel in our gut are off somehow.

In this era of artificial intelligence, bots, deep fakes, and a 24/7 propaganda machine, it may be more crucial now than ever before to return to wisdom. As we rewild ourselves, *our new stories must come from within ourselves*. We must trust the deep knowing of our sacred wild selves and honor the wisdom of the lives of beings whom we share this planet with.

Not only are we disconnected from the earth and her stories, but we are disconnected from the stories of our ancestors which were rooted in Earth story. The story of Sky Woman sparked a great curiosity in me. I had already felt drawn to my own ancestry and learned more of my Celtic roots which go back to Scotland, Wales, Ireland, and the British Isles.

It led me to wonder: What stories of creation and of the Earth have I been deprived of in my colonized existence? What did my ancestors believe before they were taught a doctrine of original sin or dispensationalism? How did my ancestors connect with the elements and with animals and plants? How much did they already know that the Earth was their home, without having to unlearn all of the terrible theology that says otherwise?

Because of my upbringing and long steeping in evangelicalism, I learned to easily dismiss other stories as myths, folklore, and fairy tales, but to take everything literal in scriptures. In order to undo and repair this kind of harm, we have to ensure we do not close ourselves off from stories as some suggest we do. Instead, we need to open ourselves up more to the possibility of the truths in the stories many of us have othered, stories which are Indigenous and land-connected. We must learn to embrace the wisdom and the beauty in Earth stories. We must honor the lessons and apply the medicine to our hearts, our communities, and to the Earth.

At a springtime Wild Church gathering, no one showed up but my family. Except, that isn't true. When I read the story of Sky Woman aloud, the maple trees around us listened as well as a three-legged squirrel who came up to our table and sat while I read. I couldn't help but be moved deeply as I read the story to this small more-than-human being and my wife and children. I wondered at his ability to climb a nearby tree. The old story tells me he's just a rodent. The story of the Earth tells me he is a beloved child of the forest and worthy of our care and love, and that he and I are deeply connected.

Perhaps, like me, you were taught the Genesis story of creation or something similar. If you haven't read the story of Sky Woman or another Indigenous creation story, I encourage you to do so right now. I also invite you to join me in the following practice for re-storying as a form of restoration of our connection to the earth and Source.

INVITATION:

Bring something to write with and some paper (a journal or any paper will do) and go outside to find a place to sit for a while. You might choose a park, your yard, the beach. Wherever you can be outside and connect with the Earth will do.

Once you are outside and settled, look around you. What plants are nearby? Or if you do not know their names, then what do they look like? What is the temperature outside? Is the wind blowing? If so, what does it feel and sound like?

What animals do you see or hear? Insects? Birds? Any mammals, fish, reptiles, amphibians?

What do you smell? What do you taste in the air (if anything)?

Think of all of these beings around you and what you are noticing. What might they tell you of the origin story? What do they offer you as a story for creation and being?

Take some time to write down any insights you have. Then write the story you are hearing from the Earth.

How is it different from the one you were taught? How might you honor and carry this story?

Give a gift of "thank you" or a song or clean up litter as a show of appreciation.

CHAPTER 13
INCLUSION OF THE WILD

It doesn't take very long to witness the sharp divides we create and the ones we perceive between ourselves and others. I grow increasingly concerned with the false dualities we have set up and which have been perpetuated (maybe more like set on fire with gasoline) by social media, consuming news and information from one-sided sources, and our stubbornness as humans.

Whether it's the narrative of us vs. them, belief vs. science, or our version of right vs. what we feel is wrong, we expect people to fall completely in line or get out. If someone is not fully with us, they must be against us and therefore canceled and cast out. Thus, accountability has fallen by the wayside, and we find ourselves in deeper trenches. Unable to see a different perspective and unable to speak with kindness or listen with true attentiveness and curiosity.

There is the truth that we need to protect ourselves and others from harm. Some people do commit very harmful actions. Hate groups and fascism are realities we face. It is true that we need safe spaces away from harmful language, rhetoric, and actions. However, I do believe that we have gone too far at times, causing would-be allies to distance themselves from us and creating splintering among even justice focused coalitions and groups. Moral absolutism, requiring full agreement on all things, has wounded our movements toward equity and justice.

The lie that we should fear each other has taken many forms, and we have not only bought into it, we have begun to follow it religiously, and of course formed our own sects and denominations accordingly, religious and not. It informs where we live, where we shop, who we follow on social media, what groups we are part of, who we will listen to, what news outlets we trust, and what books we will and won't pick up. We continue to fracture until we are cut off from most of those around us.

How incredibly unnatural and unimaginative we have become.

The wilderness beckons us to see how foolish our ideas of animosity are.

When we observe the wilderness, we begin to see how connected everything is, and how much each part is needed for life to thrive.

LESSONS FROM THE OCEAN

A few years ago, my wife and I decided to take our kids to the beach for a spring break trip. We had never visited the area we went to, but we decided to stay on a side of the beach that seemed far enough away from noise and crowds. When we arrived, we took a walk out onto the beach in the evening and realized we were next to a wildlife park. The next morning, tide pools filled with several types of herons, cranes, and pipers.

I had no idea there were so many varieties of them. As we walked along the beach, we noticed many bird watchers with large scopes on tripods, cameras with extreme zoom attachments, and vests filled with filters, guides, and small binoculars all poised to take in the diversity of birds present.

As the tide continued to move out, we could walk several hundred yards into the bay, the water only ever reaching below our knees. Hermit crabs scurried along underneath the shimmering ocean. Little fish brushed our ankles as they swam by. A large horseshoe crab meandered through sand underwater. Pelicans rested on the sea in the distance as others dove in to catch fish. Still, the sandpipers and herons stayed in the shallowest areas, digging for clams near the large oyster beds that lined great rocks. A constant movement of water filled the air with gentle lulling sound.

As I walked out in the light of the late morning sun, I stopped for a moment to take it all in, and felt a realization well up within. A very real sense of being part of this. Everything around me, teeming with life and energy, was deeply connected with me. The pelicans, the crabs, the fish, the sand, the plankton, the herons, the pipers, the water, the bird watchers and beach goers *were all connected*.

Years later, this moment stays with me, and it has changed the way I see things from my garden and forests, to our communities we are part of, to the world as a whole.

Our connections are true. Our connections are vast and interwoven beyond what we could imagine. Our connections are inextricable. Whether we like it or not. Rewilding our communities can feel as difficult as it does expansive.

REGENERATIVE FARMING PRACTICES and rewilding techniques all begin with a foundational knowledge of the power of the ecosystem. From the microbes within the ground to the grasses, trees, insects, birds, mammals, and more—all forms of life are needed for true flourishing.

Yet, we live as if we are separate.

What if we simply started talking to each other again?

I mean that. What if the time in the doctor's waiting room, the check out line, or the school function were all opportunities to have a connection with another human being? It doesn't have to be long or even the small talk that introverts dread. As an introvert who is also social, I feel drained by some small talk, but something important gets lost when we fail to acknowledge each other and instead turn toward our screens.

I recently had an interaction online where someone said "Old people will talk to anyone who will listen." I couldn't help but feel deeply saddened by their sentiment not only because of how disparaging this sounded, but also because they couldn't see the same behavior in themself online. So many people say they don't want to actually talk, yet they turn to "social" media.

We are guilty of a self-imposed isolation from people who differ from us, which drives us further and further apart and robs us of the delight and challenge of being human together. Though we are wired for connection, we tend to favor the pseudo-connection and consumption offered by social media platforms. We consume even "friendships" along with our obsession with consumption of goods, entertainment, and what we misname "living."

Have you also noticed what I have? That people don't want to talk to each other at all, despite the consistent research that tells us that connection isn't just healthy for society but healthy for the human body and spirit?

Our individualism is killing us, but we still pursue individual home ownership over living in community. We still choose technology and text over face to face and voice to voice connection. We still too often choose to stay in our own houses and consume through streaming and shopping instead of being with other people in community or being outside in nature.

Many of us even engage with nature as if the wonders of our planet are here to entertain or be consumed, instead of connecting with the trees, waters, stones, and animals that surround us. Too seldom do we slow down and listen and truly hear from these more-than-humans and let the messages sink into our skin and our hearts.

But it is the connection that each of us holds to each other, to the Earth, to the waters, to the sky that is the actual lifeblood of our planet and each of us. And in this connection, Spirit dwells.

To reconnect with how interconnected and interdependent we are, we cannot do it from the foundation of a lie. We have to be bold, speak the truth in love, and not be guilty of the same appalling silence that the Rev. Dr. Martin Luther King Jr. taught about in his Letter from a Birmingham Jail. We cannot paint pictures of unity and coming together when we deny the full extent of the predatory nature of some people as well as the stains and scars of white supremacy, patriarchy, xenophobia, and queerphobia. We must name our failures and the ways we have not allowed interdependence.

Instead, we must be honest about the harm done, and when necessary be separate while acknowledging the fact we are still connected and interdependent.

In coaching, I sometimes ask the question "What does that look like?" in order to help people I am working with to form the vision for what they are creating. Here's how I answer that question for this separate yet still connected necessity.

This looks like offline heartfelt and truthful conversations between those who advocate for the oppressed and those who continue to oppress others through their actions, votes, words, and silence.

This looks like hosting gatherings and creating communities where oppressed people are not just welcomed but *centered* in their presence, their safety, and their well-being. Which means, no—*not* all are welcome. But an open invitation exists to repentance, reconciliation, and repair.

This looks like speaking up and encouraging others to do the same, and especially elevating the voices of those who have been oppressed and listening to and believing them.

This looks like advocacy work, antiracism work, and internal work to remove our own prejudices, and education to help others do the same. It looks like equipping people to make the changes necessary to be together again.

We tend to think of inclusion as a net we cast, trying to collect as many different kinds of people as we can. Or perhaps we think of inclusion as a table we set, and that we have invited everyone to come to. But both of these are human-centric and conventional ways to think of something that is wild.

Wild inclusion is more like a field. The field the Sufi poet Rumi said he would meet us at. The field of all possibilities. But this is a field not just left to its own devices. Instead, this is a *meadow* that has lovingly been tended to as it rewilds. The native plants have been given every best chance by uprooting that which would kill them or hinder their growth. Rodents, insects, and migratory birds help with seed control, pollinating, and distribution of seeds. Waters flow above and deep beneath the surface, feeding and supporting life systems while the mycelium network below pulsates with communication and nutrients. All are interdependent on each other.

Here are some ways I believe we can remember and strengthen our interdependence:

- Reject moral absolutism and remember we need each other.
- Truly include the marginalized and oppressed.
- Create mutual aid networks that can be as simple as a group chat centered on who needs what and who can help or creating a "library" of things that could be shared (camping gear, tools, kitchen supplies, a garden, etc.)
- Support local sustainable farms and food systems if possible.
- Barter/trade with others when you can.
- Move conversations offline when possible. Meet in person or speak to each other with voice or video.
- Gather and build community in person and outdoors.

Wild inclusion includes the earth and the more-than-humans who share our home. If we do not recognize and live within the wisdom of our interconnection with all, then we seal our own doom as well as prevent ourselves from living a full and wonderful life. The following invitation encourages you to open your eyes to the ecosystem you are part of and to help it thrive.

INVITATION:

Take a look at your local ecosystem. You can do this by researching your watershed, your state or national level wildlife organizations, local conservation organizations, or at your local library.

What animals and plants are present? What are some of

their characteristics? How do they work together and with the waters and lands in your area?

Now, think about the local human community nearby. What needs are there that you know of? What needs are present in the more-than-human community in your area?

How might mutual aid with humans and the more-than-humans in your region look? For example: If there is need for litter clean up and need for human connection, could this be a mutually beneficial way to help each other?

In what ways does the local more-than-human ecosystem inspire you to think of mutual aid in your neighborhood or area you live in? What can you offer back to the land and waters to help?

To take this even deeper, go into your local ecosystem to think through these questions and listen to what the Earth has to say.

CHAPTER 14
NATURAL ORDER: COMMUNITY OVER INSTITUTION

I HOLD deep questions and skepticism for the very structure of church, the institutionalization of spirituality and religion, and the forms of leadership and systems that result from this way of spiritual community existing. The unnatural ordering of hierarchy and unquestioning adherence to tradition and policy create an empire-loving dynamic while choking out creativity and mutuality.

I believe we are living in a time when a great shift is occurring away from patriarchal leadership, empire, hierarchy, and even institution toward divine feminine, mutuality, and equitable community. I believe we are birthing a new way of being that includes some ancient ways of being, and that we are what the beloved activist and deep ecology scholar Joanna Macy calls the Great Turning. I believe we are coming back to what our bones know: *We are the Earth.*

When I observe nature, I see the Mother Tree in particular and how she sustains, cares, and communicates. Her leadership is one of listening, honoring, providing, standing in truth, and consistency. I witness the migrations of geese and sandhill cranes, forming and reforming flying Vs through the sky as they shift who takes the lead. I watch the murmurations of starlings and the flocks of chimney sweeps as they dance and swoop in the air above a pasture. I learn how in animal species where females experience menopause, that this is a time of coming into leadership and sharing wisdom.

While I hold onto the sense of comfort these bring me, I also know that the unraveling of institutions, even when necessary, will bring pain. There are comforts some of us will need to be willing to sacrifice, especially for those of us who are white and in the category of settler. I know that as I am watching the crumbling of empires and their reactive violent grasp in real time, I often find myself afraid, angry, crying for justice.

Somehow I sometimes feel weirdly hopeful and eager for what we could create if we find a way to live differently instead of relying on empire. We cannot continue along in the way we have. We must learn to live differently.

Somewhere in all of our lineages (and some further back than others) are people who lived in community and lived close to the Earth and within her rhythms. When I listen and learn from the Land Back movement and when I read through the work of The Worldview Literacy Project, which teaches Indigenous worldview, I can't help but wonder if we can move toward restoration. I wonder what it will mean for us to reclaim ancient knowing, but also what we will create and discover.

When we move beyond institution and our tendency toward hierarchy and rules of governance, we open ourselves to the alchemy of spontaneity, collaboration, and mutuality. We create more sustainable, healing, and life-giving ways to live.

When I say institution, I mean establishment with hierarchies, walls, rigid rules, and baked in white supremacy culture, patriarchy, and empire (even if those establishments claim to be progressive). I mean empire-loving and empire adjacent and obedient orders, groups, businesses, and more.

Just as many before me and with me have labeled our disconnection with nature and each other as a deeply spiritual problem, I also believe our entanglement with institution and preference for order and rulership are a deeply spiritual problem. They are all part of the same problem, that we are enmeshed with empire and all of the unjust -isms that come with it.

Even our ideas of community have been heavily influenced by our relationship with institution. We default to categorization and institutional groups when we define who our communities are. We have church communities, school and work communities, professional communities, identity-based communities, interest-based communities, and so on.

However, the call to rewild means remembering and restoring a different way to do life together. We can remember that when we are with another person, and when we are connected and paying attention to each other, *that is community*. We can remember that community does not need a label or an official document. We can practice community that has no leader or dogma to follow. We can be in a mutual relationship with others without marginalizing and gatekeeping.

As I am writing this chapter, the poet Andrea Gibson has just died, and eco-philosopher Joanna Macy is in the process of dying. I remember when another writer and teacher important to me, Rachel Held Evans, died a few years ago, and how deeply it affected me. In all of these transitions, I've been especially moved by how surrounded each of these people have been in their final moments of this life. I've found myself asking what it will be like for me and how much does it say about how someone lived when they die surrounded by love. For those whose deaths did not allow that, I reflect on how much it says when the outpouring of love and memory eclipses what seemed like finality.

In the living of our day-to-day, we can focus on building more of what empire craves: products, buildings, structures, rules and laws. Or, we can choose to create what community needs: generosity, joy, authenticity, integrity, and the safety and security of reciprocity.

We can sow seeds in gardens to create food, but also tend to the native plants and wild beings who inhabit the land. We can cultivate love, connection, abundance, and beauty that support thriving community. We can consciously interweave our lives with other people, and with the Earth.

Earlier in this book, I shared the story of standing on the shoreline and for the first time in my life being able to feel and see the interconnection of all in a vivid and visceral way. Now as I think through the idea of community, I recognize some of the ways we have gotten it wrong. In the church and much of western society, we tend to think of community as a form of institution. But also as an "it" and a "thing" we participate or do not participate in.

Instead, we must remember that community itself is a form of *life*. Community is a living entity created by intention, belonging, and being. *Community is ecosystem.*

We are already connected.

We are already part of each other and part of this Earth.

We are already existing within a global and galactic web of life.

What we must do is *bring intention and attention* to our roles and relationships. We must repair the lost conversations and forgotten wisdom. We must return to one another, to the waters, to the lands, to our own hearts, to the sky.

Joanna Macy's incredible life work, The Work that Reconnects, refers to the Great Turning, a movement away from our late-capitalism and industrial growth-based society into a more sustainable and life-nurturing society. Within this work is awakening to the fact we are the Earth and deeply connected. From many Indigenous cultures throughout the world, we see time and again the teaching that we are all one.

One of my favorite stories relayed by Andrea Gibson during their cancer treatment talked about how their father woke up one morning to find he had lost one eyebrow. Andrea so poignantly suggested this was so they wouldn't have to lose theirs due to chemotherapy. This story of interconnection has stayed with me.

Living in this time when crisis after crisis comes to our attention, I see that we are also being reminded with each new heartbreak that we are inextricably connected with each other and with this planet.

As the wheels of institution unravel and we begin to turn in new ways, the heart of being able to make it through this is to do it together. With other humans, with more than human beings, with our ancestors, and with our descendants in heart and mind.

I would be lying if I told you I don't sometimes wish I lived in another time or at least in another culture with more people who "get it." But the more I lean into the possibilities and the ways I already witness this turning, and the more I recognize that time itself, as a kinship view reminds us, is not linear but cyclical, the more I know my being alive in this moment is a good, hard, beautiful, severe, and sacred thing.

Joanna Macy said that she prefers the term *unravel* over the term "collapse." *Unraveling* helps us understand the ways that these unsustainable systems are turning and loosening. I see the church unraveling, and not just unraveling in the ways that many within the deconstruction movement have suggested. I see the ways that empire-influence has been woven in, even with what I once thought of as progressive. I have witnessed firsthand the corruption of hierarchy and wall-building and gatekeeping.

I don't think that this is how it was supposed to be.

Though my own beliefs have changed drastically, I still find beauty in reading about the early church, groups of people meeting in homes, not trying to overtake anyone but trying to remember their teacher who was murdered by the state. I find beauty in how wealth was distributed enough so there was no-one among them who had need. I also find beauty in reading the rhythmic practices of my Celtic ancestors, gathering and living together along with the seasons and turning of the Earth.

As I have wandered and wondered my way outward and into a more wild and free spirituality, I have found a much deeper resonance in practicing a more natural form of together-ness. I have found deep beauty and wisdom in learning of other intentional gatherings and groups practicing this way of being together and in relationship with each other and with the Earth. I feel drawn and invited to continue creating more and joining more wherever and whenever I can.

Institution would have us isolated and tethered to addictions and materialism. Community and kinship invite us to solidarity and interweaving with sharing and simplicity. This industrial growth society has glorified technology and hacked our attention. Life-nurturing community calls us to remember the glory of nature and to restore our attention to where it belongs.

So where do we begin? How do we nurture this communal way to live and go through this time of the unraveling together? How do we create community without hierarchy and gate-keeping?

I believe the most helpful thing we can do is to practice the world we want to create with the people we are connected with. I know the most practical way to begin is to not be lost in the research, but to invest our energy in our own living. In doing life together and bringing intention and attention to our interconnectedness, we create the inroads to communal life-nurturing society.

There may be times we ask "who is in charge" or wonder if we should ask for permission. There may be times, a lot of times, when things get messy. We will grieve. We will rejoice. We will rediscover what it means to return.

INVITATION:

This practice invites you to use your moral imagination as well as to open your heart and mind to the more-than-human community around you.

You've already been asked to research your local watershed and ecosystem. Recall what you learned about how the beings in your area work together to create life-sustaining society in the natural world. It might be particular plants and animals having symbiotic relationships like pollination, seed carrying, and habitat.

Knowing this, and considering this Great Turning toward life-sustaining society: What do you imagine if everything works out? What if we do get it right as humanity? Then what does community look like? How do we live together?

What can we do now to turn toward this way of being in community? How can you practice this in your own relationships?

CHAPTER 15

REWILDING AND DECONSTRUCTION

I USED to believe that what we now often call deconstruction was the beginning of a process of faith unraveling and re-examination. I used to think this was a first step before reconstruction could take place. I believed that if we wanted to reconstruct and reclaim, that we would need to do so after deconstruction and some healing time had taken place.

Likewise, as a therapist trained in trauma work and specializing in helping people heal from spiritual trauma, I believed the work of re-examination served as a prerequisite. I thought that if we wished, we could rebuild from the rubble left behind. After all, spiritual trauma has a way of scorching and destroying so much of our spirits and spiritual lives that they often become unrecognizable to us.

Now, though, I realize that a healthy and robust spirituality is not an add on or option to pursue after the unraveling or post-healing. Instead, it's the way through.

We've had it backwards for too long, and this backwards positioning has led to a deep severing for many people between their spirits and the rest of themselves.

Rewilding our spirits and attuning our spiritual selves to deeper truth and connection offer us a new construct, or way of thinking through and viewing spirituality. It is through this new construct that we can more clearly discern what is a helpful versus a harmful belief. More than that, though, rewilding also calls us to get out of our tendency of being stuck in our heads, attune to our heart-wisdom and knowing, and to be in our bodies, outside of our individualism. Instead, we are invited and called to remember we are an embodied part of something larger: the Earth, an ecosystem, and a Universe.

We are called to community and remembrance of who we are and our own agency.

The ideas of deconstruction and reconstruction constitute a removed and human-made colorization of what is a deeply intimate and natural process in spiritual development. Much of the discourse and teachings perpetuate this approach and in so doing create more rage, dis-ease, and resentment. Even the many social media accounts mocking evangelicals continue to establish an order of us vs. them and an outside authority determinant on what is acceptable and what is not, while stirring emotions. Entire platforms and social media empires thrive on keeping former evangelicals especially in these states of dysregulation.

But the Earth invites us to regulate. To ease our breathing and to simply listen and know.

From this knowing, we can see it is not so much about deconstructing or re-constructing anything. Institution and constructing is what got us in this mess in the first place. It's more about returning, unlearning, relearning, being, and releasing. We can better see it is not just about our individual selves. It's also about *us*.

In giving a presentation about spiritual trauma in therapy, I was asked how I would define a healthy spirituality. Through my years of my own spiritual wrestling and unraveling and recovery from spiritual trauma and my experience in helping many others through their own, I would offer some simple suggestions. A healthy spirituality includes self-agency, an understanding of our interconnection, a rejection of hero worship or following a talking head, and an embodied living in community and in the Earth.

A more natural process of growth seems to fit better for getting to this: evolution. We do not tear down and start from scratch. That's impossible, no matter how much we might want that to be true at times, and no matter how it might feel when we've been laid to waste by spiritual abuse. Instead, we learn. We adapt. And when we take to heart what we have learned, we grow into a wiser version of ourselves. We evolve in context, in connection, and in community.

When we see ourselves as part of both literal and figurative ecosystems, it changes how we view our own evolving. Rewilding ourselves involves returning and remembrance, but it's also and perhaps more about moving forward from where we've been.

We move forward.

We now know what we once believed was progress is actually regression. We recognize the warning signs, the red flags, the tell-tale markers of empire and control. We are attuned to the ways we've been conditioned and indoctrinated. We can see with clarity what supremacy and colonization have stolen from us and our neighbors and the Earth.

Perhaps, most importantly, we know there is a better way. And we know not just what we are moving away from, but what we are moving toward.

We move through.

We move through the current hell-scape of sociopolitical disasters and violence. We move through the work of decolonizing our viewpoints, our systems, and the way we relate to the land and waters. We recognize the ways we've inflicted damage to the Earth, to all inhabitants of Earth, and to ourselves. We are deeply attuned to better ways to exist and thrive, and we embrace them as we move through the messiness of changing the way we live.

Where much of the popular deconstruction movement calls us to more individualism and a continuance of supremacist and colonized understandings, rewilding calls us to each other and to belonging within the Earth. Where some would suggest we must reject spirituality outright and others that we need to believe in particular and prescribed ways, rewilding reminds us that no-one can or should prescribe belief. And rewilding calls us to radically accept all of our being: body, mind, spirit, and relationships.

Rewilding invites us to listen. To listen to others' stories, to the trees, to the river, to the wind, to the birds and the animals. And to listen to the spirits, including our own.

When we gather for Wild Church, we do not listen to one person giving their individual thoughts. It's not that there is no sermon. It's that the sermon is sacred conversation. No one person has the answers. No one being or species carries the truth to be disseminated to the rest of us. Instead, all are invited to speak and be heard. We sit in a circle, and we make agreements to listen with respect, with understanding and compassion, and to hold our own views lightly. We do not give advice or prescriptions on living or belief.

Instead, we bear witness to each other, from the youngest child to the eldest adult and from the smallest hoverfly to the greatest oak tree. We honor and believe in the wisdom of the collective.

When I first experienced a crisis of faith after leaving an extremely abusive church, there was no terminology, much less an entire movement with social media platforms, podcasts, and dozens of books. Instead, there were scant documentaries on cults, a website from a cult deprogrammer, and an earnest prayer in the dark of night—which was more of a question and wondering. In some ways, I envy the amount of resources available, but in others I worry about the continued problematic ways that many in this movement perpetuate the same harms people have experienced from the evangelical church. Even while writing this book, there have been exposés on big names and leaders accused of the very abuse they claim to help with. I've even found myself on the receiving end of online abuse and vitriol from some exvangelical writers and personas.

More and more, I am learning to not put faith or trust in any one person or even movement. I am learning that if I do that, I certainly will be let down. That's a very hard lesson to learn, since I was conditioned to unquestioningly be a follower. But I *did* start to ask questions. Then I started to learn that not only can I *ask* questions, I can *answer* them. And I can get answers from sources which may have been forbidden before. I can receive answers from people who believe something I don't. I can receive wisdom from the spirits of the forest and ancient traditional knowledge which might have been labeled as "of the devil" in the denomination I grew up in.

If the ideas of deconstruction and reconstruction have been helpful for you, I would never tell you to reject them. If it's been a lifeline for you, I'm so grateful. But if you feel like there's something missing or you've been wounded by the modern movement and its talking heads, I invite you to listen to what rewilding has to offer you. If you are curious about what spirituality could mean outside of dogma and religion and prescribed belief, I encourage you to take that curiosity outside.

I believe the lines we've drawn around what is church and faith and belief will continue to shift and even blur. More of us recognize the unsustainable nature of how we've been organizing spiritually. We see the gaps and the missing natural world, as well as the ways we keep repeating the same mistakes and perpetuating rather than rectifying and healing harm.

What I most hope is that we move beyond the right vs. wrong and us vs. them rhetoric and beyond the activating ways we keep each other angry and grieving and resentful. I hope we move away from dialogue that creates more distance and instead embrace a vocabulary that brings us closer to ourselves and to each other and the Earth. I hope we move forward and through, toward a more embodied and wilder way of spirituality and being human.

INVITATION:

Earlier, I talked about the need for creating and engaging in healthier spirituality at the same time as re-thinking, that this is the way through trauma and what we often call "deconstruction."

Take a walk where there are plants, whether it is the forest, a field, your yard, or a local park. Notice where the ground is and how much the soil is covered. Where soil gets bare, something often fills the space. What is best to be in that place is a native plant or a natural mulch to help the soil.

Look into the native plants in your area. Can you plant something native? Can you volunteer to care for a native patch at a local park or farm? Can you care for the soil and many creatures by creating a pile of wood or an area you can let be wild?

Once you have recognized what you can do, do this with the intent of recognizing you are building the future and partici-pating in a better way. This is the same with our spirits when we engage in a healthier view and open our eyes to what is helping vs. what is harming our connection and living in sustainable ways.

CHAPTER 16

PREDATORS

> *Beware the wolves in sheep's clothing, yes. But also the ones who want to eradicate the wolves, the wildflowers, and wildness of all kinds.*

It doesn't take long when talking about wildness and wilderness, that someone brings up danger and inevitably the topic of predators. Wild Church cofounder and author Victoria Loorz does a wonderful job highlighting how often humans think of consuming other animals as normal, yet will noisily protest the idea of having predators near us who might see us as prey.

The fear of predators stops many people from going into wild places, even when encounters with them are relatively rare. The lethality and power of such animals can be frightening, and it would be foolish to suggest we have nothing to fear or to discourage caution. Of course, we should be aware of our surroundings, aware of predators in the area, and also respectful of them.

As a kid growing up watching the *Discovery Channel*, I

always hated the moment in a documentary about animals when a zebra or antelope would be brought down by a big cat. I remember wishing that they were herbivores, too. But now that I'm older, I understand a little better, even though I still do not want to watch it. Predators are necessary in the web of life.

If you have never listened to the TED Talk or read about the reintroduction of wolves at Yellowstone National Park, I highly encourage you to take the time. Understanding predators as a vital part of the ecosystem offers us a much-needed perspective shift and a deeper appreciation for animals we may have been taught to fear or even despise.

But I can't stop thinking, every time I start to address the idea of predators, that the focus is displaced.

THE MOST DANGEROUS PREDATOR OF ALL IS (IN)HUMANITY.

Old growth forests are clear cut. Colonization continues to destroy natural areas. White supremacy, overconsumption, and patriarchy fuel a form of capitalism that dumps chemical and animal waste in Black neighborhoods and plastic in the ocean, while keeping diverse voices silenced. Data centers poison water basins. Factory farms pollute the air, land, and water—harming rural communities and the rivers nearby.

But it happens on an individual and a local level, too. Sometimes by the people we are supposed to be able to trust. Sometimes by the church. Sometimes by someone closer to home.

My grandparents lived on a hill overlooking the Tennessee River, and many summer evenings were spent with my parents standing on the riverbank and casting lines into the brown muddy water. The smell of the river still takes me back to many fond memories, including walking with my grandmother along the riverside, watching my grandfather tend to his bee hives, and peaceful, languid days of fishing, woodworking, and gardening with my calm and quiet grandparents. The space they offered contrasted sharply to the loudness I experienced in the Pentecostal church and to what often happened at home.

It was at that spot on the river that I learned how to skip a stone on the surface of the water, how to bait a hook, how to use a bamboo pole, and how to watch for water snakes. It would be the spot I would stand at as an adult, knowing it would be the last time as my grandfather slipped away from this life after battling cancer.

Despite the goodness, I can still recall the worst time spent there, even feeling it in my body, clenching against the violence and eruption of rage.

During an evening fishing with my parents and brother, my mom's line became taut, and she reeled in a fairly large fish—one she was proud of, the kind you hope to catch when you are into fishing. As would normally happen when one of us would catch a fish, my dad took the pole and began to work to unhook the fish's mouth. But instead of putting the fish back in the water, this time he threw the fish to the ground. He took up a large piece of tree limb and began thrashing it into the fish's body as the fish writhed and jumped around, desperately trying to get away as we screamed and pleaded for him to stop. But he didn't.

He took the bloodied still fish and threw it into the river, murmuring it was a drum, full of bones and white people didn't eat them. We *never* ate fish from the river. The waters had long been polluted in the 70s, and this was late 1980s or early 1990s. Even as a child, I saw through to the truth of why he did it: racism (white supremacy), violence, rage, disdain of the natural world with an air of entitlement, and of course, patriarchy.

I recently went with my children and wife to the Tennessee Aquarium in my hometown of Chattanooga, and as we were reaching the end of the freshwater building, I noticed some fish sucking up stones and spitting them back out. These bottom feeders were close, and through the thick glass I watched them closely for a while, admiring their understated beauty and the motions as they kept the bottom of the tank clear. Then I looked to the plaques to see what kind of fish they were: freshwater drums.

What some, including my father, have failed to see is the horror and moral failure of their actions toward this world and the inhabitants who dwell here. For too many people, the world is here to be used, misused, and even exploited. Their theological (mis)understandings include that the world is temporary, that God is not in or of the world, and that the world is somehow opposed to her creator. They also fail to see the beauty in what they fear or despise, and they fail to experience the joy and connection we can have with more-than-human beings.

As a queer woman brought up in the south and the Pentecostal church, I know all too well about the predators running rampant in the church and in religious spaces.

The sad truth is that many come to spiritual and religious leadership without healing their own wounds. Many come to lead without any training on boundaries and healthy leadership styles. A lack of true accountability pervades church cultures where pastors believe they have "the final say" and other church leaders pass on a top-down approach even when it's supposed to be more congregational. Some people take on leadership roles out of their desire to dominate, control, and even abuse. No church culture or tradition is exempt from this. These kinds of predators exist everywhere, and unlike natural predators, they are not vital to the ecosystem. In fact, they can destroy it, and often do.

Because of the pervasiveness of hierarchy and lack of accountability, religious institutions are often fertile ground for abuse to form and be normalized.

But in the Sacred Wild, this kind of forming and normalizing of abusive behavior cannot thrive, because it goes against nature. The Earth gives us examples of leadership and co-living which exist in strong relationships, symbiosis, and reciprocity.

AFTER DOING the work of helping others heal from spiritual trauma for over 15 years, I've become increasingly interested in how we prevent this kind of trauma and how we can engage in spirituality that is healthier, non-dogmatic, and non-hierarchical. How do we fight against predation within spiritual spaces?

I can't stop thinking the answer might be the same as how we fight against the predation affecting our Earth: Divest/Reinvest, Mindfully Assess, Accountability.

If we are to stop the predation of unrelenting and greedy capitalism, we have to divest from the capitalist systems harming our planet. It means not over consuming, buying only what we actually need, and using our resources as a form of investing in the future we want instead. That might mean supporting local farmers, artisans, shops, non-profits, and mutual aid. It might mean bartering and trading, as well as living more communally.

Similarly, if we want to stop the predation in churches, we have to divest from those systems. It might mean removing membership, tithes and offerings, and followership on social media as a form of divesting from institutions that have or are causing harm. It might mean taking our bodies, our money and time, and our attention to community building, to nature, and mutual aid. It means interweaving with what is life-sustaining and builds on justice and positive peace.

We have to assess and be honest about what practices and systems we are engaging in and the lifestyle habits we have that contribute to the harm of the environment. Do we purchase factory farmed meat or sustainably farmed or eat plant-based? Do we purchase fast fashion or highly durable clothes? Do we use AI or write the email the old-fashioned way? Do we buy second-hand when we can?

Do we think about how our actions and our daily choices impact other people and the planet?

Likewise, we need to consider what practices and systems we participate in spiritually which might perpetuate harm. Do we sing songs and hymns that are rife with patriarchy, supremacy, and control? Do we ensure our language is more inclusive, or do we revert to traditional language? Do we continue to invest in hierarchy and institutionalism over community and movement? Do we create mass amounts of waste in church or spiritual community via paper, plastic, and energy use?

Do we even think about how our spiritual practices might impact other people or the planet?

Finally, we must stop predators through accountability. Accountability for inhumanity that harms the Earth includes fines, legal charges, and restorative actions from those who have caused harm. But if we stop there, our accountability suffers from being reactionary. We need accountability in the form of organizing that works to stop the exploitation before it starts, as well as accountability within ourselves and our communities. What structures and boundaries can we put in place? What protections are possible, and how do we actively participate in creating safety and care for the waters, lands, and all life?

Several countries have implemented rights for nature, a wonderful example of such protections.

We need similar accountability in spiritual communities. Yes, we need sanctions and often even legal actions. We need restorative actions from the perpetrators and enablers of abuse. But we need to think proactively and form boundaries and structures and communal participation. What can we do to actively participate in creating care and safer community? What kind of community structure and model do we need to prevent abuse and dominance?

As we work toward rewilding, it will be ever important to be aware of the predator of inhumanity within ourselves, within our communities, and within the world. The next reflections offer you some time to think about your place in the web, as well as your role in ending unnatural predation within yourself and within communities you may be part of. These can be very helpful questions and thoughts to bring to friends, a community you are part of, or a discussion group.

INVITATION:

In recovering from my own spiritual trauma, I often have found the wild places offer me gentleness, restoration, and a sense of being held. I also see so much potential for how the natural rhythms and orders in the wild can guide us toward ending unnatural predation and upheaval. As you are thinking through these questions with me, I invite you to take these reflections and the following practice and reflection to a natural place you feel held by, if possible, or at least a place where you feel safe.

Look around you when you are in this place. What is there? Who is there? Notice the Earth supporting you beneath you. How does it feel to sense the Earth beneath you?

Are there any trees or stones nearby that offer a sense of sturdiness? Anything offering you peace or a sense of calm?

From this state, think about how you might Divest/Reinvest, Mindfully Assess, and discover what Accountability looks like to stop unnatural predation. Be sure to talk through these with people you are in community or relationship with.

CHAPTER 17
LIFE IN THE BRAMBLES

WHAT ABOUT THE MARGINS? What about the beings who tend to be on the periphery?

All too often, in ways both literal and figurative, native plants like chickweed, plantain, and the blackberry thorns and brambles which sprawl freely upon the land are looked down upon, uprooted, and destroyed. They dare to grow on the fences, next to buildings, in abandoned lots, and in backyards. Most commonly, they grow in the margins.

Of course, as a queer woman from the south and raised in the evangelical church, the word "margins" has a significant meaning and history for me. But I've noticed a significant shift in how I see this language.

I was listening to a podcast not long ago where an author I respect and admire discussed being in the margins as a gay man and loving other people in the margins. This is, of course, something many people have said and something I have even felt and identified with at times. But in that moment, something in me resisted the word "margins" for the very first time. I've come to realize in the past couple of years that it's simply not good enough.

I don't believe that viewing marginalized communities in this way of "people in the margins" is especially helpful. And I've come to believe that even this language continues harm already done, even when we don't realize it. After all, it is often not by choice that we are banished to the margins.

But more than that, I've come to understand a deeper truth. We don't actually reside in the margins, at least not for long.

Instead, *we are the wild ones*, those whose home is most found *in the wilderness*. We may visit the margins of institution, looking for connection or to share truth. But the wilderness provides the place where we feel the most free.

It has always struck me how in many epic tales like *The Chronicles of Narnia, The Lord of the Rings*, or *The Hobbit*, there is a moment when the main characters visit someone who resides in the very areas considered dangerous to cross. Whether it's in the home of the Beavers or Tom Bombadil or the forest of Lothlorien, adventurers find shelter, friendship, rest, rejuvenation, and often wise counsel among those who more readily inhabit the Wild.

In *The Hobbit*, one such character, Beorn, embodies mystery and danger. Yet Beorn carries a harrowing and heart wrenching story of being forced into exile after a genocide left him a sole survivor. A "skin changer," or person who can shift into an animal, this BearMan demonstrates what it means to inhabit the wilderness as a place of safety, and how dangerous the institutions can be for those who are deemed "too different" for whatever the reason.

Perhaps the most faulty assumption with talk of "people in the margins" is to think that we would all desire to be brought into institution. Instead, for many of us, we know the peril of hierarchy and the corruption of money and power. We know it best because we have been most wounded by it in churches, governments, businesses, and more.

We instead long for more people to come and know the safety, beauty, and freedom here in the Wild. We yearn for the creation of community independent of control, dogma, rules, and strangling structure. We know that the best and most vibrant connections are those found when we deepen our connection with the Earth and fall into her rhythms and songs.

As I write this, I am walking through my own latest spiritual trauma, this time at the hands of a once progressive church which my wife and I had been part for over a dozen years. Deep disagreements with the latest pastor over her lack of acknowledgement of injustice and concerns of the queer community, racism, and a disgustingly weak response toward Christian nationalism led to more disappointment and harm. An unhealthy obsession with creating a church where the affluent oppressor could feel welcome along with the oppressed took precedence over the church's rich history of standing up for justice, even to the point of being firebombed for integrating during segregation.

As I grew more uncomfortable with this institution while serving as a music minister, I started recognizing my own deep discomfort with institutionalism in general and my longing to be free from it completely (though on my own terms, not in the way that happened which caused harm to me and my family). In one of our final disagreements before my position was taken away from me with no notice, the minister told me I needed to realize the job I was doing was institutional work.

Music, creating, and leading people in songs that move them to connect and inspire them to act is *never* the work of institution. Poetry, song making, and singing with heart will always be *wild*. Unless we choke all the life out of musical expression and make it become formulaic. Much of the mainline tradition continues to do this. Then inadvertently (or perhaps in some cases purposefully) they ostracize artists, creatives, and would-be allies for the sake of bringing in traditionalist people who have more money to give. Sadly, in a trend toward more conservative ideology and voting among mainline Christians, we see the fruits of that clinging to archaic and harmful language and tradition. Meanwhile, the change-makers and edge-walkers are pushed away.

The wild among us, like the brambles, are feared.

We cannot be controlled.

We reject the unnatural order and placement.

We grow and roam.

When we are cut back, we grow again.

And spread.

But what if, instead of fear, we were met with the same wonder some of us experience when we walk along the fence line and watch for the ripening blackberries at the end of the thorns? What if more of us realized the safe harbor the vines of brambles give to rabbits, birds, and caterpillars metamorphosing into butterflies?

What if we wild ones were valued, protected, and even revered?

Who might come out and meet us, stay awhile, and hear the songs and tales we might share to help them on their journeys? What delights might the weary and rejected come to know if they knew that *beyond the margins* is the *true expanse* opening into abundance, deep connection, and richer way to live?

For this to happen, it will require the work of perspective taking, moving outward, and detoxing ourselves from empire, colonialism, and supremacy culture.

In working toward decolonizing ourselves and seeking restorative justice, the need arises for de-centering. De-centering means to remove what has been centered (often white heteronormative maleness) and instead center the ones who are not typically included. At first, that might sound simple, but the work of truly de-centering requires us to leave the spaces we occupy and shift into new ones. It requires us to move outward instead of inward, downward and deeper, more intentionally. It means admitting and correcting our wrongs and being willing to be corrected. It invites us to listen instead of speaking, and to listen without formulating a response.

The work of de-centering means also removing privileged and rigid leadership and instead replacing it with minority rooted, communal decision making. It means restructuring and moving away from patriarchy and hierarchy and other hallmarks of empire toward beloved community and more natural ways of leading and serving. It means expanding rather than contracting. It means replacing top-down teaching with collective wisdom.

Most challenging for some of us, we will need to do deep inner work to decenter whiteness, maleness, heterosexuality, binaries of many kinds, and other ways we have come to center in-power people and experiences. This inner work means recognizing what we have internalized and how those things show up in our thoughts, our reactions, our opinions, and then our actions and complacencies.

Only from a place of true de-centering can we have eyes to see and ears to hear that we've been missing what we should have noticed all along. We've replaced sacred, wild being with obsession over in-group being and with institutional alignment.

For too long, too many of us have placed our hope and allegiance in institutions rather than each other. We have obsessed over rules, dogma, and power structures while romanticizing monarchies and lordships. Nowhere is this more clear than in the language that dominates the western church in prayers, hymns, songs, and scripture readings. Dominion language squashes the voice of those in the wilderness, preferring ruling instead.

To create a rewilded way of living, we must replace our trust in institution with a trust in ourselves, in each other, and in the Earth and more-than-humans. Nature has no institution. Instead, nature has an ecosystem. And as we know, institutions so often wreak havoc on the natural ecosystems.

By walking outside of institution and recognizing the wisdom outside of what we have put so much trust, money, time, and belief in, we can then open ourselves up to a deeper knowing and richer way to live, like the wild ones in the world know.

The morning glories on the edge of my garden bloom at daybreak.

They ask you and me to do the same and wake up to the day with opening ourselves.

The river flows freely where the dam has been removed, reaching and fertilizing the ground.

She asks us to free up ourselves and move with the Earth instead of against her.

The mockingbird mimics the calls she heard in the night, even the whippoorwill.

She invites you and me to listen so well that we can recall another's voice.

The woman I know who reads cards and the Earth to gain wisdom invites me to learn to read these things, too, so I can be in touch with more knowing. *I invite you to come listen, too.*

The truth is that the truth does not belong to one group.

It never has and never will.

Instead, there is an ever-expanding field, and the ones who love the field and live in that prairie best know what it means to truly thrive. Maybe if we listen and learn, we can know, too.

INVITATION:

In this practice, I invite you to shift your perspective. What animals or plants in your area have you considered to be a nuisance? Perhaps it's a dandelion that keeps coming up in the driveway. Maybe it's a group of crows or a patch of brambles. It could be a spider who builds her web on your porch. Pay special attention to what is on the edges.

Take some time to sit with or observe these beings who make things untamed, messy, or different than you intended.

What do you notice about them when you look up close? What might you appreciate when you look with different eyes?

What do you notice about how they exist within the web of life and the ecosystem?

To take this further, what do they model to you about inclusion?

Give thanks and honor them by letting them be or offering water, attention, or care.

CHAPTER 18
NO CREATURE TOO SMALL

Because I've known what it's like to be misunderstood, unwanted, and seen in a negative way, I tend to delight in many species seen as pests and those who've had their beauty overlooked. I love to watch crows interact with each other and listen to the many different sounds they make. I often marvel over spiders, especially orb weavers of any kind and their intricate and spell-binding webs. I can lose myself in a bed of moss or tiny wildflowers like field pansies, cranesbill, speedwell, and henbit.

Something about the way nature is often ranked by us humans reminds me of the social ordering that happened in middle and high school and somehow continued on into workplaces and the accompanying politics. Popularity, image, and "it factor" take precedence over goodness, kindness, and even talent.

We gravitate to the highest summits, the most panoramic views, and the highest waterfalls, but we ignore the understated quiet beauty of undergrowth wildflowers, simple trails among tree trunks, and gentle paths which lead us to wander into "thin places" where the worlds of spirit and Earth are more permeable.

Somehow, we prefer eagles and forget kestrels exist. We obsess over nature docuseries and even travel distances to see certain species while neglecting the creatures and wonders in our own backyards.

The mundane and familiar remain overlooked. But this is also the place where miracles and water-to-wine magic tend to occur. Tiny wonders lie at our feet, beckoning us to see them and to bear witness to their own miraculous nature.

While reading *Braiding Sweetgrass*, I found myself captivated by Robin Wall Kimmerer's telling of lying underneath a fallen tree to watch how water drops form on moss. Not only did it lead me to pay more attention to water on moss, but I found myself drawn to this level of attention and devotion toward something so overlooked. I also wondered to myself: Did the moss know Robin was near? Did the moss feel the level of care and attentiveness of a woman lying under a fallen tree in the pouring rain?

I found myself paying attention to an unlikely creature early one summer. I had just watered my seedlings, and among the run-off a red wasp perched on the edge of a tiny pool. I stood still and watched her stand on the edge, dip her arms in and pull them up toward her again and again. I admit, it astonished me when I realized what she was doing: taking a bath.

I laughed at first at how absurdly cute a wasp bath could be. But then I felt grief for how I had wasted so many years of being afraid of or disdaining these creatures. For those of us who grew up in the country, wasps were often seen as a nuisance, and their nests sprayed with cans of pesticide made to eliminate them. In that moment of watching the little wasp take a bath, I made a decision to act with love toward them.

Now, I've seen the wasps pollinating plants in our garden. I watch them take baths in the bee bath I made for them and other pollinators to enjoy. I've accidentally brushed a few while picking fruits and have not been stung. The more I tune in to their small world, the more I seem to appreciate them and something within myself that I have not yet been able to name.

In another moment of noticing, my family visited a local zoo. As we passed by a couple of local birds, I noticed an American Crow behind the wire. I stopped and looked at him a moment and smiled. As I took a step closer, my kids and wife moved in toward his cage, too.

"Hiiii!" I offered him a little greeting in a cheerful voice.

"Hiiii!" He answered back, repeating not just my word and tone, but also my attention.

My family gasped and laughed, and the crow moved closer to the front of the cage and pushed his head through as far as he could, wide-eyed and curious.

He didn't say anything else to us, but he stayed focused on me. I wondered how many people notice him and how many people just walk by. We had walked by other times. We see crows every day. But this encounter reminded me that every day is no less wondrous.

In rewilding ourselves, it becomes key to open our senses to what is already around us. For me, it's the snails, the cedar trees, the ferns, the oaks, the blackbird and sparrow. I have a deep affinity for the phrase "no creature too small" because I am learning more and more how connected we are and how important all beings are in our Earth. It hit home even more when I met a small creature in need.

One morning, I felt a prompting to go outside for a walk. I took my normal route winding around our barn and coming by our garden to walk by Grandmother Pecan tree and back to the house. When I neared our pecan, I saw something moving on the ground. It was grey, soaking wet, shaking violently, and trying to walk. As I got close enough, I realized the something was a baby opossum.

Unsure of what to do, I called my wife, D.

Why? Because this woman adores opossums. I'm talking has-opossum-shirts-level adores them.

D gave me a couple of ideas, and we called someone local who we knew had rescued and rehabilitated orphaned opossums. I scooped her up, wrapped her in a towel and held her close to try to get her warm and dry. She was covered in fleas and continued to shiver for a while.

Over the next few hours, with a warming pad, towels, and watchfulness all directed by Sam, the rescuer, the little one—who we started calling Trudy—started to become more active. We got in touch with a rehabilitation center who had room for her and got her to safety and care.

Little Trudy left a mark on me, so much so that a song came to me that was a commitment to care "For Every Creature." I can honestly say I never thought I would be inspired by an opossum to write a song, much less a song that's deeply spiritual or for group singing in a spiritual community.

Only a few months before this, I watched helplessly as someone sped up to hit and kill two of our ducks who had wandered into the road. No one pulled over to help me or even slowed down when they passed as I wept and retrieved their lifeless, wounded bodies from the road. Why have people become so cruel toward animals? Why do people mock those of us who go out of our way to treat animals with kindness and respect? Why are online vegan and vegetarian spaces trolled by people intent on killing and eating animals and people who have no empathy for the animals unjustly and mercilessly tortured in factory farm settings?

These are questions I pondered on for weeks after our ducks were killed. So when little Trudy showed up, it felt like a nudge from the Divine to live out this conviction to better care for animals and to create something to help raise consciousness in myself and others. The experience moved me to think about how we might pray and sing for caring better for all of the life in this world.

The first step to this kind of care is to open our eyes and see what we may be overlooking.

TINY WONDERS. I keep repeating the phrase.

The words come to me like the gentle flow of a soft creek or brook.

Where my feet touch the ground, all around there are wonders. Some of them are so small, that I must bow to the Earth to notice them.

As I walk in the dew-soaked grass with a new song in my voice, I notice a shift from the general to the specific. I hear the sound of the sparrow singing in the morning, the gentle consistent hum of insects and the rustle of breeze in the leaves. I see two crows in the distance, landed on a hill. I witness a blade of tall grass wave to me as if inviting me over to make contact. So, I do.

The many greens of the grass and prairie plants permeate me along with the blue of the sky. It's here that I can no longer take it and loosen my sandals so that I can stand on the holy ground in a few moments of silence and awe.

My feet in the cool and recklessly damp grass and earth, I become acutely aware: The Divine Mystery is with me. The warmth of morning sun touches my shoulders and bare arms, and I open my hands and raise them. I close my eyes and see the red orange of the inside of my eyelids as I turn to the East.

Over the next several minutes, an outflow of love, protection, and boundlessness radiates from my heart and across my lips: a Seven Directions Prayer. I turn in each direction, my full body activated and present.

It's when my last words are spoken that I look down again, considering my sandals and if I should put them back on. But instead my eyes are drawn to the web.

Minuscule silver strands sparkle in the sun between grass blades. Dew drops hang and play in the light and on the breeze.

And here in this tiny wonder, I find Her. I see Her glowing and thriving and dancing. I hear Her invitation to dance, too. And to recognize the wonder that I also am.

INVITATION:

For this invitation, stay close to home. Be outside somewhere you are frequently, in your yard or a green space or natural area you visit often. Maybe it's on the edge of a parking lot.

Close your eyes for a few moments and take some deep breaths. When you open your eyes, imagine you are crossing a threshold into the more-than-human world.

What specific* plants and animals are present? What trees are present? What ground level plants? What birds do you hear or see? What other animals? Insects? What stones and fungi are at your feet?

Choose a small wild one to observe for awhile.

Open your eyes to this small one's way of being. Notice how this wild one is present. Notice how they exist within their environment and the web here in this space.

What tiny wonders are there with you? Take some time to

simply be present to all of the everyday miracles so often ignored. And let them stay with you as you come back and cross the threshold back to your living.

* You might want to use a field guide or app like Seek by iNaturalist or Merlin Bird ID if you are unsure or still getting acquainted with the wild beings in your area.

CHAPTER 19
POWER OF THE WILD

As HUMANS, we have a tendency to give our power away. From an early age, we are taught to discount our inner wisdom in favor of trusting adults and what they teach us. Teachers, supervisors, parents, and other authority figures silence us, causing us to question if we truly have knowledge or wisdom within ourselves. Or worse, we believe we are wrong and always need guidance. We need to recognize this grooming and programming which comes from many directions in order to keep us under control and tamed.

Our authority is given away at the workplace and within our capitalist culture that demands using our time and energy for productivity and paying taxes. We make ourselves subordinate to people paid more than us, even when they have less experience, knowledge, or skill. Somehow, the titles and hierarchical structure train us to believe we are less worthy, even when we hold resentment about it.

On a larger scale, we give our power away when we accept unjust laws, inept and corrupt leadership, and the desecration of our lands by corporations. For centuries, atrocities have been committed against Black, Brown, and Indigenous peoples in the name of the law. Instead of massive uprisings and putting our bodies on the line, many of us, especially those of us who are white, are taught to submit to the authority of the law and to obey.

Spiritually, we submit ourselves to pastors and leaders instead of recognizing that Spirit lives in us and in the trees, waters, sky, and all beings. We too easily relinquish our own spiritual agency as we buy into the lies after lies we are sold that we need an expert, a guru, a pastor, and even a savior. We buy into the narrative that we are not good, that we are broken, incomplete, and weak. We learn to distrust and discount our own inner voices, bodies, and heart wisdom. In evangelicalism especially, but also in other western Christian sects, we've been conditioned to seek rule by a king or lord and to bend our knees to dominion.

Our time of reclaiming our own power, including spiritually, is now. The reclaiming of our own authority and power is a brave, revolutionary, and deeply spiritual act.

To become our fully sacred wild selves, we must stand up and use our voices, our bodies, and our minds to reclaim our own authority and agency.

No more should we bow to so-called spiritual authority.

No more should we allow ourselves to be manipulated by institutions designed to control and subdue us.

No more should we repeat the harmful messages that we are unworthy, undeserving, or not to be trusted or listened to.

We will and must remember who we truly are, awaken to our full selves, and start living in this remembrance and return.

The same Spirit which breathes inside the lion and the condor and the honeybee resides in us.

The same divine mystery dancing on the wind, rolling in the waves, and stretching through the branches of trees animates our being.

We are made of the same stardust as Jupiter, Arcturus, and Vega.

Our voices hold the power to soothe, to heal, to connect, and to bring down tyrants.

Our siblings are the mighty cedar, the soaring hawk, the rolling river, and the whispering grass in the field.

We are children of the Earth and of the Universe.

We are sacred.

We are wild.

When we recognize our wild selves, we recognize our power: muscle, endurance, flexibility, courage, and strength.

But also wisdom, kindness, kinship, community, rootedness, and warmth.

We hold within us the power to create and to bring destruction. For much too long, we've followed the script of destruction rather than creation, especially when it has come to our planet.

We have given our power away to corporations, to corrupt leadership, and to outside authority. We have learned to default to the greed and whims of others instead of acting in ways that are in the best interest of humanity and of the Earth and all beings.

What if we leaned into our own power instead and created energy solutions which are clean and renewable?

What if we used our strength and endurance to demolish unnecessary structures and reforest and re-wild areas that have become abandoned concrete, brick, and wood?

What if we leaned into our wisdom and stopped overconsumption in favor of simplicity, natural beauty, and connection?

Through our own innovation and courage, we can plant trees, cultivate food, cut the cord with controlling tech, and turn to each other and the natural world instead.

We are living in a moment which is the precipice for remembering our own sacred, wild power. We are beginning to awaken and reconnect with the knowledge and strength of our ancestors and of the Earth-centric cultures of the world.

I RECENTLY WENT for a swim in a lake with my friend, Aline. Perhaps, swim is a stretch. I only go where I can stand in the water. I have never been a good swimmer, except for one summer vacation when I somehow got good enough to swim in the deep end. But because I stayed out of practice, I have stayed in the shallows.

I long to put my body in the depths of the water, but first I will need to remember my own wild power. Though it is hard to believe, I know it is in me.

My grandfather swam across the Tennessee River as a young man in an exercise to prove his strength. I've always found this to be so poignant, because this wild swim saved his life at two other points. Once, when fighting in World War II, he swam across a river away from enemy forces and to safety. Another time, after I was born, he was caught in a great landslide that pushed his car into the river. He was found clinging on to a tree he swam to.

How is it that his descendant could grow up afraid to swim? How could I have been so separated from the water that I grew to fear her?

I've been saying lately that I have a complicated relationship with water. Remember when I told you I'm a Cancer sun and rising? And that I'm a Pisces moon? That's a lot of water. I love the water. I spent a lot of time on the banks of the Tennessee River as a child. But now I long to be *in* the water.

Now I yearn to let the river and the lake hold me. Each time I lay back and lean into the power of the water to hold me afloat, I release more of my limiting beliefs. I come home to the memory of my own power balanced with the power of the Earth.

As women and as people who have been marginalized for one reason or another, we especially have had our power drilled out of us. We've learned songs, scriptures, teachings, and unspoken messages that have built up in our hearts and minds like a slow poison. It's time to detox.

Reclaiming our power will require us to cleanse the rivers of our minds and spirits. We are called to listen to what the trees, rivers, oceans, and stones have to say to us.

We are invited to recognize our names in birdsong, in the wind whispering through a forest, and in the stars dotting the night sky.

We are not sinners. We are not broken. We are not incomplete.

We are powerful wild beings, filled with the same animating life force that turns worlds into orbit and pulls the ebbs and flows of the ocean tides.

One of the most harmful aspects of spiritual trauma, especially in that which is covert or embedded in the teachings, is the loss of personal authority and agency. *Power.*

If we have had this kind of wounding, our healing also needs to include reclaiming our power through exercising agency and personal authority. We do this through practicing decision making, taking stands in advocacy and justice work, and learning to trust our inner voices again through listening. We do this by ceasing to feed ourselves the messages that instruct us to surrender our power. We do this by reminding ourselves of a new narrative, that we are wonderfully made. We do this by living in that fullness and wonder.

May we wonder at the power of our hands, to push seeds into soil and cultivate gardens of beauty and nourishment. To create music and art. To hold and to touch.

May we wonder at the power of our feet, to traverse landscapes unknown to us, to scale rocky terrain, and to cross waters. To kiss the ground as peace activist and poet Thich Nhat Han encouraged us to walk.

May we wonder and fully lean in to the power of our voices, to say "no more," to encourage and inspire. To sing and create beauty in the air. To express and to proclaim.

May we live in the fullness of the power of our hearts, to experience both love and heartbreak, to connect with the earth and with each other and Spirit. To pump and sustain. To know and be known.

I hope we live fully in the wonder of the power our bodies and minds and spirits. That when we walk, run, climb, swim, create, touch, kiss, connect, reflect, sing, and dance, we remember just how powerful we truly are.

INVITATION:

Take some time to reflect. Notice the power around you in the natural world.

It might be in the thunder clap. It could be in the sturdiness of a tree or resiliency of a native plant. Maybe it's in the way a flower seeds itself so it can grow again next year. What about the way a bird takes flight? Or the way an animal runs?

What power and agency do you notice?

Now notice your own power. You, too, are nature. What stood out to you near the end of this chapter in wondering at our power? Which of these would you like to practice?

Would you like to take a small action? You have the power and the freedom to choose.

CHAPTER 20
REWILDING WORSHIP & SPIRITUAL COMMUNITY

As WE RE-WILD the world and our spirits, we must not forget to re-wild our spiritual communities, the ways we gather, and even how we think of worship.

Too often, we subdue the wildness of Spirit and the creative dance of the Divine by closing ourselves off from risk taking and newness, and from embracing full diversity in our practices. Making the circle ever wider and less defined feels threatening. What if it bursts?

But perhaps the more frightening question is: *What if we are trapped in a bubble of our making?* What if we are limiting and harming ourselves as individuals and as a community in our short-sightedness?

By re-wilding our communities, we strengthen the bonds we share and make our groups more resilient against the diseases which have taken hold in many spiritual groups and churches. Diseases we also tend to face in society: greed, racism, queerphobia, complacency, isolation.

When I look across a monocultural field, I notice how

"dead" it seems. Sure, there is the green of the corn or soybeans or hay. But only for a while. Sooner or later, the season will shift. Harvest will come, and then the green will give way to emptiness and decay. Below the surface, if herbicides and pesticides are also used, even more threats to life are found in struggling microbes and a lack of mycelium and connections.

Meanwhile, in the forest and even in the edges of the fields where the trees, shrubs, and wildlings grow, a consistent cycling of green and liveliness thrives. Birds build their nests here and find food and rest. Butterflies and bees feed on the nectar of tiny wildflowers. Scurrying mammals make homes in fallen logs and stones, and the deer find refuge from the sweltering sun and food to sustain them.

In my experience of church, there was too often the pressure and the expectation to be monocultural. This applied to what I read, what I listened to, what I believed, how I worshipped, how I spoke, and who I associated with. Even within my last experience in a mainline church, tradition and dominant culture somehow reigned supreme over justice and protecting marginalized community members who bring newness and change.

Unfortunately for many communities, this refusal to shift, expand, and rewild spells out death. This death might be the slow decay of losing vibrance. It might be the loss of integrity or the loss of trust which has become shattered. Room is given for abuse of power and for the perpetuation of religious trauma.

Rewilding, like the strength of a garden full of variety offers spiritual community the protection and support that only diversity can bring. When Spirit is free to move and guide, we are called to adventure and find refuge in the not-knowing. When we engage with Divine Mystery, we tap into our own potential and glimpse into the unboundedness of true divine love. We realize the strength in expansion. We recognize the need for wild ones, for mystics, poets, prophets, dreamers, and artists. These *edge walkers* invite us all to something more vibrant and sustainable.

Fear keeps us insulated in our sheltered monoculture versions of church. Fear keeps us singing the same lyrics and worried to change our tune. Fear blocks us from taking a strong stand against oppression. Fear keeps us from boldly proclaiming extravagant welcome beyond words by embodying allyship with our lives.

But love?

Love calls to us from the deep recesses of the forest. The deep green of moss and the shade of low-hanging branches whisper possibility and beckon us to come sit awhile. Love invites us to rest and listen, to take a chance and open our eyes to all that is already here around us. Love beckons us to adventure and to dream and scheme in tandem co-creation with Creator. Love opens us to see the possibilities and encourages us to take action. Love empowers us to embrace the Wild and in doing so, we become even more loving.

The cycle begins again, growing upward and outward, like a great oak tree.

Wiser. Stronger. Resilient. Wilder.

From that place, we can reconsider worship, which I define as the ways we honor, offer reverence to, and connect with Source/Spirit/Mystery. In order to reimagine worship that is rewilded, we have to both re-center and reclaim the wild.

Centering the wild requires us to remove ourselves from the center of our worship. We must take a close look at our why, our how, and our where in order to better understand who or what we are *actually* centering in our worship.

Starting at the age of fifteen and into my forties, I served in a music leader role for many settings including churches, youth rallies, chapels, and spiritual retreats. In all of these experiences, there has been an expressed preference by leaders of the institution for style, genre, and believe it or not, sometimes even tempo and key.

Controlling what is played and how it is played is just one example of how much we center ourselves in worship, no matter what the lyrics we are singing say. We can sing of focusing on Spirit, justice, or love, but in reality we are often focused on our own comfort, preferences, and satisfaction. This type of centering stems from a colonized and tamed approach to engaging with Spirit.

To make matters even worse, a further centering happens when we value performance over presence.

Instead of a turning toward each other, toward Spirit, and toward the Earth, we turn to watch and clap and say how talented we think the person performing is. Instead of centering the community, we spotlight a few. Instead of welcoming every voice, we want to see credentials, education, and an audition.

To add more trauma, the lyrics we sing find their way into our cells through the vibrations of our voices. Some of us have even learned to sing by singing songs which teach us to distrust ourselves. Lyrics encourage us to believe we are not worthy and that we are undeserving of goodness. We have been singing mantras that do more harm than good.

How can we expect to invite the wildness of Spirit when everything is about control, order, and pleasing ourselves? How can we claim that we are engaging spiritually when we are being so measured? How can such limiting and harmful practices bring about any healing or hope in a world already fractured and full of exclusions and barriers?

Re-centering the wild means not just centering the wilderness, but also the wild nature of Spirit/Mystery *and* reclaiming our own wild nature. By its very definition, we must let go of control, curation, and anything resembling colonization.

This means welcoming every voice, embracing spontaneity, and remembering that perfection is the enemy of good. It requires us to be in the moment, fully present to ourselves, to those around us, and to our environment and the in-between-ness. It means looking back to our ancestors more ancient than walls and dogmas and remembering who we really are.

We are good. We are the Earth. We are each other.

Reclaiming our wildness might feel counterintuitive when we've been indoctrinated to believe our bodies and minds are bad or somehow against our spirits. We may even react viscerally when we think about letting ourselves be wild and free. We often have been told not to trust other people who are free spirits and taught to look down on them. Taming and silencing ourselves, for many of us, has become equated with right living.

Yet, in our collective lineages, somewhere back in our ancestry are people gathering together and singing with abandon. Perhaps they are sitting or dancing around a fire. They may be baking bread or harvesting crops together. People sang together in everyday life and in ritual with each other. Using our voices in song allows us to access a primal and intuitive part of ourselves that is often squelched by society, institution, and empire.

For those of us who have been silenced, using our voices offers a powerful way to reclaim what is rightfully ours.

Just as it's important to re-story, we must write new songs and engage in music making that is fully embodied, present, and more concerned about getting connected and in the present moment than about getting it right.

Not only have modern religious traditions disparaged ancient and Indigenous beliefs, but also ancient and Indigenous practices like drumming, chanting, and singing that is focused on connection and celebration. Our focus and definitions of worship and community singing have moved from something that was wild, holy, and free to something that is tamed, controlled, performative, and even mundane.

Have you ever mumbled through a hymn at a service?

Returning and remembering worship as participation, honor, revering, and responding to the Divine/Spirit/Mystery would help guide us back.

If we expand our ideas beyond seeing "God" as an old white man sitting on a throne demanding obedience, it frees us up to remember who and what we are truly honoring when we worship. What if we instead focused on sacred unity, the love that flows in and between all things, mystery, the numinous? What if we focused on our connection with the natural world and with people around us? What if we saw Spirit in all things and all people?

How different would our response be? How then would our lyrics, tones, and rhythms rise from our voices, hands, and feet? Would we then recognize the deep connection and become more aware of the eternal presence? Would *we* then be more present instead of engaging in rote and stagnant routine and start engaging in ceremony that is life giving? Could we see ourselves more clearly and recognize our own participation in the divine?

I most wonder: Could we then collectively heal?

What if something intangible and mysterious happens when we gather and focus on something together as a collective?

There is a concept I have found myself captivated by since learning about it. When we are in groups of people and we sing collectively and with feeling, a new entity emerges known as collective effervescence. This concept conceived by sociologist Émile Durkheim helps us to understand that a special energy becomes present when we engage in activities and rituals as a collective.

When I think of this phenomenon and reflect on what I've come to understand about Spirit, I believe this mysterious connecting and tangible energy *is* Divine Mystery. The collection of our own spirits connecting with each other also connects with Creator to create this tangible entity.

This is a much wilder, more alive, and more inclusive way to see the Divine.

I cannot help but wonder if in this mysterious presence, can we heal the ways we've been taught to fear each other? Can we move closer to understanding how our actions have caused pain for other people and the planet? Could we then see more clearly how to do our part in restorative justice that makes it right for the ones who have been wronged?

All of these are important ways to move toward rewilding our worship. But bringing more wildness to worship cannot stop there. To move toward an even more wild, alive, and inclusive way of gathering, we need to expand and include the more-than-human. We tend to over-focus on bringing in and neglect the importance of moving outward. We need to move toward the Sacred Wild.

By moving outward, not only do we more effectively create a wider circle, but we also remove ourselves from our short-sightedness and self-imposed limits.

Especially within Christianity, the focus on bringing others into the circle prevents the dynamic reciprocal influence that is possible. For those of us from that tradition, we have to unlearn the notion that we should not be affected or changed by others. We have to unlearn the idea that "we are right, and they are wrong, and we need to draw them in." We especially have to unlearn the admonition that we cannot move outward unless it's to bring someone in.

The fear of being influenced by others limits our own spiritual growth and well-being. It also prevents us from listening deeply as we preoccupy our minds with our own thoughts and rebuttals.

By moving beyond our impulses to proselytize and evangelize, we open ourselves to deepen rather than impede our relationship with Spirit, each other, and Earth.

I offer an invitation to you to rewild your worship by starting with listening.

Listen to others. Listen to the more-than-human others. Listen to place, the birds, the plants, the stones, the water, the land.

What have we been missing that we can now draw our attention to? What whispers or shouts, cries, or joys can we hear?

Listen without overthinking.

Then, and only then, I invite you to sing.

I invite you to sing with attention and reverence for the wild ones.

To honor and be present.

To place participation over perfection.

To connect and move outward.

To reclaim your voice.

To be embodied and move.

To be a little wild.

INVITATION:

As you may have noticed, there are some songs I've created to go with this book. Go outside. Listen and sing along. The song lyrics are located in the end, under "Dirt Church Hymns."

I also invite you to reflect while outside: What have we been missing that we can now draw our attention to? What whispers, shouts, cries, or joys can we hear? How can you bring your community and worship to the wild?

CHAPTER 21
OPENING

As WE TALKED about with worship and gathering, so much of westernized Christianity concentrates on bringing people in, which often turns into an obsession with numbers and increasing them.

On the surface, it might look like expansion and growth. But what do we miss out on and limit ourselves from when all we do is go out in order to bring in? What are we preventing ourselves from seeing when we solely focus on a vertical and increasingly concentrated way of relating spiritually? What if instead of constricting, we expanded?

Going through adolescence in the 1990s, I remember the many object lessons, human video skits, t-shirts, songs, and youth group sermons about being separate from the world and keeping our hearts protected as we went out to try to win souls for Jesus. I faithfully bought into every single one of them, repeated them to friends, wore the shirts, and sang the songs.

By the time I had survived a couple of incredibly abusive religious experiences within the Church at large, I started wondering if this centering and obsession with church life was healthy in the first place. Only after further diving in and unraveling for years did I begin to see a deeper truth—that I had also limited my own heart and mind.

When I go into the wild, or when I simply stop and look up at the night sky for longer than a minute or two, I can't ignore the limitlessness. We are part of a Universe which is ever expanding. If you have ever deeply looked at a tree, even one that is older, there are still signs of expansion in the lighter green tips of new shoots and leaves in the summer. The roots and trunk of the tree also continue to expand, ever reaching and growing outward. A trip to the Lake Quinault area in Washington let me know just how limitless a tree can be when I stood beside the world's largest Sitka Spruce, a tree that's grown for one thousand years in a temperate rain forest.

Somewhere along the way, we started equating expansion with danger. The wild itself became a place in our minds full of traps, terrors, and even seduction away from truth and wisdom.

But this is a vastly different view than the wisdom of our ancestors and those who lived more closely with the rhythms of the earth. Throughout the world and in many cultures, wisdom bearers from shamans to prophets to healers to even Jesus himself spent time going into the wilderness for more communication with Spirit. Instead of a place of danger, the wild was known to be a well of wisdom, support, and deep spiritual growth.

In the colonized West, we've been primed to think wisdom comes from the written word, from people who are in positions of authority, and from institutions. We've also been conditioned to believe there is a split between what is sacred and what is mundane, causing us to miss the holy other. Expanding our view of what is sacred helps us to break free of some of these limits we have placed on ourselves.

Perhaps, the beginning of expansion happens below the

surface, the deep mycelial networks of the forest floor, the microbes in our garden soil, and the stirrings and awakenings in our own hearts.

One of the most beautiful ways we can begin to expand beyond our limited and constricting views and ways of being is to intentionally open our hearts. It is in the subtlety that we can best expand outward. Many spiritual teachers suggest that spirituality is really open-heartedness, open-mindedness. It doesn't take long to witness closed-mindedness and closed-heartedness in the world. We have a tendency to shut out, shut down, and shut off when we face a person we disagree with or a concept we don't like.

I also believe this gets taken even further when we over-analyze and when we stop at the point of deconstruction with no movement toward rebuilding or reconnecting. Perhaps this is most apparent in spaces where spirituality itself is rejected with no room for nuance or perspective taking.

We all have a spirit, and we can all choose whether or not we connect with the depth of ourselves, with other people and natural life-forms beyond humanity, and with Divine Mystery. It is through this reconnection that we can heal our own disconnections and isolation.

If spirituality is open-heartedness and opening our minds, then wild spirituality is the opening of a door to relationship with the wild. The wildness in our natural world, the wildness within ourselves, and the wildness of Spirit, Divine Mystery, Source.

But we must realize that opening is not a two or ten step program. Neither is it a one-time choice.

Rather, opening our hearts and *choosing to keep our hearts open* is a daily, hourly, and even minute-by-minute practice. And when we have closed our hearts for a long time, it makes the opening of them feel more frightening and even elusive. Sometimes, heartbreak leads us to close our hearts out of self-protection.

For too many of us, we have been taught that love is limited and deeply conditional. We may feel silly or even like something is wrong with loving a wild being or a wild place. We may have been deeply wounded by someone who said they loved us or betrayed by someone we loved. Maybe we broke a promise to someone we loved. Maybe our hearts feel incapable of love.

Loving does not require us to do more than we can do or to have more than we have.

Loving does require us to be. To embody love by being present. Loving requires us to know and to allow ourselves to be known. When we are loving, we listen, we see. And when we are loved, we open up to be heard and seen, just as we are.

Our family recently went on a ride in our VW Bus. It's a fun way to spend an hour or so when the weather is nice, just to ride around in the countryside with the windows down. Apropos of the 1960s and 70s era these buses hail from, our bus is adorned with many bumper stickers that make strong statements. Our daughter read one aloud while we were riding and asked what it meant: "Minds are like parachutes. They only function when open."

As we responded to her about the importance of being open to others' perspectives and being willing to change our minds, I couldn't help but think about how much of my life I believed the opposite of that. I believed that minds worked best when closed down, ready to engage in debate and apologetics, and ready to sway others to believe the one absolute "Gospel truth."

I once feared being open. From what fundamentalism taught me, openness would lead me astray. Openness would mean abandoning Jesus and everything he stood for. It would lead me to destruction, to embracing sinfulness, and to losing salvation, especially as a queer woman.

Now, I realize none of this is true. But there is a kernel of truth that opening our minds is a dangerous business. When we open our minds, we cannot go back, not really. Everything will be made new, and we will see how much more is unknown. We will see how our closed mindedness has actually limited us.

For me, my own openness has meant accepting myself as a lesbian and embracing the beauty and wonder of how I am made. Opening my mind and heart has also led me toward more openness with how I listen to others and to hold more lightly to belief and convictions. Becoming more open has awakened me to wonder and to more curiosity. And openness had led me to a wider and deeper love.

So with wild spirituality (the opening to relationship with the wildness in our natural world, ourselves, and of Source) I also recognize that love leads the opening. When love leads us, we have a tendency to open more. When we are led by something other than love, whether it be fear, hatred, or aloofness, we have a tendency to close down.

It might seem like circular reasoning. We need love in order to open. Openness leads us to love.

But I am coming to understand this process is more like water. Water moves within, upon, underneath, and over the land. Water cycles, rising from the ocean into the clouds, falling on the ground, seeping into the soil, running into the rivers which spill into the ocean.

Like water, the cycle of love meets us at many points, leads us to moments when we are awash, and guides us through moments when only deep groundwater carries us through. Beginning with a small surface trickle or sprinkle of rain, love carries on to an ocean of depth.

What does it mean to let love open us to relationship with sacred wildness? What does it mean to open our hearts and live open heartedly? What does it mean to open our minds and let them function like parachutes as we launch from the cliffs of what we once thought was safety and realize limitlessness instead?

Like water, love begins in a quiet and seemingly imperceptible moment in a particular and singular relationship. Love that has the power to form canyons, fill oceans, and nourish the land begins with a drop or a trickle.

I have witnessed the power of this kind of love that meets a single moment in a particular relationship in my own friendships and even in momentous connections with strangers. The power of love opening a heart in the same manner that water finds its way has been most evident in my moving through the world as a queer person.

Time and again, I have witnessed the opening of minds when people listen without formulating response or argument. When students, staff members, healthcare workers, and nonprofit leaders hear a part of my story or meet me and really see and hear me, I've heard the unlocking of closed-down minds. I've known love to take friends on a journey from knowing to accepting to celebrating, then to advocating and allyship. That journey began with a conversation and an unveiling that allowed more love.

In opening to the Sacred Wild, we also must begin a conversation. Only this time, our role is to listen and bear witness to the stories around us of the kin we've failed to recognize.

The particularity of relationship might be a single tree, a certain animal, or a specific place. For many of us, it might even be easy to think of a wild being we have loved. For others, because of our socialization to believe in our separateness, we will need to cultivate relationship with a particular wild being or wild place.

Living with openness will require us to move beyond that particularity and to adopt a stance of staying open. We will need to practice opening our hearts when they want to shut down from fear, grief, and exhaustion. We will need to continue to open our minds and practice holding our convictions lightly when we want to tighten and clamp down on what we think we know.

When so much around us has been crumbling, I often get the sense we are on a precipice which feels ominous. I do not know what lies ahead. I only know that the very foundation so many of us have been standing on can no longer hold. I know that we have stayed on this unstable cliff for too long, ignoring the warning signs. I know that it is time to launch away from how we've been trying to do things, to do life. In order to survive, we need hearts and minds open like parachutes to carry us into the limitless nature of what lies ahead. I only know that it is through love that we will open ourselves to each other and to Spirit, the Earth, and our own hearts.

INVITATION TO OPEN:

Do you have a wild being you already have a connection or relationship with? A particular tree, animal, plant, river or other body of water?

Can you be with that wild being for a while? Or if not that wild one, then please choose another you would like to connect with and form a relationship.

If you do not yet have a relationship with a wild being, please choose one which you can see or be near fairly often so you can cultivate a relationship. This is about deepening a connection over time.

When you are with this Wild One, listen. What do you notice them saying or doing? What do they need? Look deeply. Notice the aliveness in them. What do you appreciate about them? How might you love them better? How can you show your love?

CHAPTER 22
REWILD THE WORLD.
REWILD WITHIN

THE MORE I consider the importance of rewilding, the more I wonder what kind of renewal is possible in our spirits and even our bodies when we allow the rewilding process to take root within us. Would we rediscover wonder? Could we re-engage long forgotten and atrophied muscles that could be rebuilt? Could it be that our liberation is not just tied up with each other's but also with the Earth's?

I believe the answer to all of this is a resounding yes.

In *Braiding Sweetgrass*, Robin Wall Kimmerer brings up an idea I have been meditating on ever since: becoming indigenous to the land. She goes on to explain that this way of living means caring for the lands and waters "as if our lives, both material and spiritual, depended on it."

The call to rewild resonates in these words. Over the past couple of years I have embraced this call more fully, and I have found this deep connection of my own liberation and the liberation of communities and the waters and lands to all be deeply connected.

In fights against the factory farm industry from further

poisoning the river and land for our neighbors, and in recent wins from Native Nations which have led to liberation for land and for people, the connections on a material level are obvious.

On a spiritual level, I notice as I put in work to rewild our yard that I can be near-sighted and underestimate what it will take. It isn't enough just to remove some invasive species. It isn't enough to scatter wildflower seeds. It takes both a wide and close view. I have to think of the dirt, the insects, the plants, the light, and the water.

In my own process of rewilding spiritually, I have learned this wide and close view helps me stay away from the individualistic tendencies I learned in evangelicalism. It's not enough to just tend to the thoughts and perspectives I need to weed out. It's not enough just to plant new and better beliefs and practices. I also have to tend to the ecosystems of my community, the lands and waters and more-than-humans I live with. I have to draw out the white supremacy culture like the poison it is and apply the medicine of reclaiming what colonizing and empire took from my ancestors and from me.

This work is both deep and long-form.

But it is also immediate and transformative.

This is necessary work for all of us who live within the systems of empire. Whether we were exposed to the harms of fundamentalism or not, we all have work to do in reorienting ourselves to the Wild and wild spirituality.

Conventional modern living, and all of the comforts that come with it continue to draw us away from what our ancestors once knew and what we would also know if we lived closer to the Earth. This is why rewilding the world around us is key to our process of rewilding within. *We are the Earth.* Therefore, when we rewild our yards, a field, or a parking lot, we rewild ourselves, too.

Rewilding often means rule breaking and going against the

grain of what we've been taught. HOAs, city codes, and housing situations need some updating and catching up to support wildlife habitats, no-mow yards, and other rewilding efforts that can be done at home. Sometimes, this means getting in touch with the courage our tamed living has snuffed out.

I often wonder how many of my ancestors did it. I have grandparents who survived the Great Depression and WWII. I have ancestors who walked up and down an Appalachian mountainside in the dark in order to get to relatives and church services. I can't seem to imagine possessing their level of bravery.

In my own process of rewilding, I am working on building my courage when it comes to water and heights, and a camping trip gave me an opportunity to work on getting more comfortable with water.

I took our kids to meet up with friends and camp near a trail I used to hike regularly. Though I'd been to the lake there often, I had never gone out on it. My friend Aline had her canoe and offered to go out together near sunset. I must have looked especially tense, gripping the sides of her canoe as we made our way out on the water and she switched to using a trolling motor. She asked me several times if I was doing alright, and offered lots of reassurances.

After we had glided out a while, I started taking in the sound of the water gently sloshing against the boat, the colors in the sky, and the scent of the water that reminds me of home. We made our way into a small cove along with another friend, Naomi, and her son. I watched in delight and a bit of awe as her son swam in the open water.

When it was time to head back, we noticed something ahead of us in the air. Soon we found ourselves surrounded by a swarm of mayflies. They cascaded out of the woods, their beating wings creating a chorus of sound as thousands of them took flight. Some of them were mating while others flew about, and a few of them landed on the water to be eaten by fish.

As we sat there watching in wonder, I couldn't help but think what an auspicious moment this was—to happen upon a swarm of insects that are alive in this way only for a moment. Watching them while sitting on the open water called me to the edges of comfort, fear, and adventure. I began to recognize that it's in these wild encounters and in fostering these wild lives that we ourselves become rewilded and re-attuned to the rhythms and mysteries of being alive in the Earth.

Our collective liberation and our rewilding are bound up together.

I do not think I have to tell you how much our lives and the lives of many species depend on a turning of the tide in how we live in Earth. Like many who pay at least a little bit of attention to climate justice, I have nights when I lose sleep over my deep concern and grief over the state of our planet and the losses of life and habitat we have experienced. I grieve for the old growth forests I will never know. I grieve for what was lost long before I was born. I grieve for what we are losing now.

We took our son to a science museum, and at the end of the fossil section, there is a sign that shares about the loss of the great giant animals due to a predator who hunted them to extinction. To see this predator, you must slide a door. Behind that door is a mirror.

In rewilding our lives, we must also take action with what we know now. We humans have over-consumed for far too long. We have not lived in harmony and balance for much of our existence. Our current way of life is completely unsustainable for humanity and for the more-than-human beings who call Earth home.

Still, I am determined. I see climate news of what many countries throughout the world are doing. I see nations in Latin

America and throughout the world taking a lead in recognizing the Rights of Nature. I see scientists engineering more sustainable ways for construction, discovering ways to get rid of waste, and creatively capturing water and creating clean energy. I see Native Nations bringing lawsuits and winning conservation cases that have impacts long past the local place they are protecting.

I see more awareness of the problems with fast fashion, factory farming, over-consumption, and AI data centers. I meet more people intent on living in sustainable and life-giving ways. I get to know more people intent on being The Great Turning.

I also see a movement of people who are restoring the connection between nature and Spirit. Many of us are reclaiming the wisdom of our ancestors and seeking better ways to live in deep relationship with the Earth.

Environmental activist George Monbiot gave a brilliant TED Talk called "For More Wonder, Rewild the World." In it, he talks about ecological boredom and how rewilding can lead to a richer and rawer life.

I deeply believe this is also true for us spiritually.

As we rewild more of the world and more of ourselves, we will begin to experience a life and a spirituality that is much richer and rawer.

We will collectively start to hear and answer the calls to adventure and courage. We will trade our fear and distrust of the Wild for a deep love and loyalty.

We will regain connections we've lost and relearn how to relate to ourselves, others, and the Earth.

We will expand our creativity, our wisdom, and our empathy.

We will relearn how to be in reciprocal deep relationship with the Sacred Wild and return to wonder.

INVITATION:

I invite you to be outside and hopefully with other people if you can be as you work through this reflection. If not, be intentional about including the wild beings around you and listening to them.

Journal or discuss:

What do you feel called to rewild within yourself? Are there any particular fears or limits associated with the natural world that you feel drawn to shift?

What around you calls to be rewilded? Any areas that have been tamed or restricted? Any opportunities for some native plants or converting a small area to a pollinator garden?

What ways would you like to implement living closer with the Earth?

CHAPTER 23

WILD FAITH

> The Aramaic word 'haimanuta' is the word for 'faith' (one's confidence, firmness, or integrity of being in Sacred Unity; a connection of the sacred life force through its many outer forms in a way that is rooted, renewing, and healing; a sense of certainty or rootedness).
>
> — NEIL DOUGLAS KLOTZ

As I SET out to write this book, I had not planned to explore the topic of faith. Yet, I find myself pondering on it more and more. Through all of my wondering and deep questions, I started to recognize the strong connection between faith and finding Spirit alive in the wilderness.

It has always fascinated me that the gospels are laden with Jesus comparing the kin-dom of God and faith to mustard seeds and yeast.

When I look back to my earliest learning on this, the small mustard seed was emphasized in having enough potency to move mountains, and the lessons I was taught focused on having enough faith.

As I grew more and began accepting my own queerness, I took a new perspective of seeing mustard seeds and yeast as sometimes unwanted things, things that spread rapidly and are outside of control. Living things that bring about transformation even when they are undesirable.

Yet in this moment, I see more.

I notice the wild and free way the mustard seed is scattered and the way it flourishes without constant tending. I see the way in one parable of Jesus, the mustard seed is said to grow strong and tall, enough to be a tree and a home for birds. Impossibly so, because this is not the way that mustard grows. Wild faith defies what we might think is within reach.

I notice the way that yeast is present in the very air and flour itself, in no small part thanks to my own sourdough making. I recognize that invisible and subtle yeast spreads throughout and transforms the dough to make it rise, somehow creating more just from its untamed presence. Expansion. All it needs is the right environment to thrive.

Perhaps the point Jesus was making was in the *wildness* of it all.

At the beginning of this chapter is spiritual teacher and scholar Neil Douglas Klotz's translation of faith from the Aramaic, confidence of being in Sacred Unity, rootedness.

Perhaps when we have faith in this way, we transform ourselves and the world around us into a refuge and food for the hungry. Perhaps by rewilding our spirits and our ways of honoring Spirit, we create networks of wild being that move mountains. Perhaps this is what it means to embody wild faith.

What if this is true for enacting justice from ending hunger to enacting racial, gender, economic, and sexual justice? What if this is even and especially true for restoration and healing of the Earth?

What if it is through this *wild faith* that we can heal our waters, lands, and the climate? This is a faith that is active and living, rooted in deep connection. Confidence and deep understanding in our Sacred Unity would motivate us to more action, more love, and more living in harmony and immersion with nature.

I wonder as I look out across the green of my yard, full of what my favorite herbalist calls "wildlings" but many refer to as weeds. What if the answer to so much is here?

Answers about diversity, thriving, and flourishing in wildness.

Answers about what it means to not just accept the outcast and unwanted but to *center, honor,* and *interweave* us into common life together.

It's in this wild scattering and cooperative becoming that refuge is born for more life, for every creature.

We recently fought another industrial poultry farm from being built in our community. Our local government lifted what was a moratorium on allowing Concentrated Animal Feeding Operations in our county, and the repercussion has been dozens of these sites taking over the lands in the years since the lifting.

A groundswell of everyday people have begun to use our voices and speak in opposition as we seek to conserve and protect this area. Yet those in authority and those with power and money are doing what they can to push new factory farms through.

This is a moment when wild faith empowers us as we spend late nights researching the watershed and hop on calls with local residents and national advocates to do what we can. The Sacred Unity becomes more and more tangible as we listen to people we normally would disagree with, and they listen to us—a couple of very progressive lesbians living in a very red area. Somehow knowing we are also uniting in this cause with people from all over the watershed, the state, and the country reminds us we aren't alone, and that we are part of a much larger movement toward sustainable agriculture that feeds without destroying. We are part of a movement to restore, rewild, and reconnect.

After my last experience with institutional church where we lost a great deal and experienced much pain and trauma, I felt disillusioned and disconnected. I had been dipping my toe in the water with the Wild Church Network and had even held a Wild Church inspired gathering at our home for the Winter Solstice. I noticed there was an online Wild Church gathering I could log into, and though I had seen them available before but not attended, I answered the invitation, this time out of my own yearning and heartbreak.

So on a winter Sunday morning, I bundled up, poured a cup of hot tea, and went to sit outside with my phone tuned in to a zoom call.

What followed was no small miracle. I suddenly could not feel disconnected, even if I tried. A woman in the Netherlands read poems, led us in invitations to connect with the Wild, and asked us to share. I felt the inextricable interweaving between my heart, the Wild, and the people not just joining in to the call, but to all those who connect with the Sacred Wild. And even more widely, to all people and all beings.

Where I had felt myself falling, I felt caught and held in loving embrace. I felt loved and held by the people joining in, but also by Grandmother Pecan in our backyard, by the ground beneath me, and by the steely winter sky.

In the past, when I left the cultish church I was part of, I lost friendships, a sense of community, and for a while, my faith.

This time, I still lost friendships and a sense of community, but I gained a new one and experienced a growth in my faith which had already shifted away from progressive Christianity and toward a very expansive openness to Divine Mystery and Spirit in all things. As I've connected with the Wild, my sense of wild faith has deepened and opened new worlds of possibility, connection, and love.

I am still new to facilitating Wild Church, but I have already witnessed a more beautiful and resonant way to be in spiritual community—one that has not hindered my faith, but grown it, watered it, and allowed it to thrive in its wild and holy state. I have found others who experience the Sacred Wild and honor her, even though when I first started writing this book, I had no idea there was such a movement toward eco-spirituality.

I deeply believe that moving our faith into the Sacred Wild will deepen and strengthen our rootedness in our Sacred Unity. I also believe that this rewilding of faith will empower us to unravel the institutions which are rooted in othering, supremacy culture, and destruction. It is the rewilding of our faith that will guide us in creating culture, true community, and new ways to live with each other and in the Earth.

Faith will no longer be a statement of beliefs listed on a website.

Wild Faith will be the living connection with the waters, land, and each other.

Faith will no longer be a doctrine or list of rules.

Wild Faith will weave lovingkindness and restoration into our interactions and decision making.

Faith will no longer designate who is in and who is out.

Wild Faith will maintain our inextricable connection of kinship with all.

I once had "faith" that I was born in sinfulness and that I needed a savior and bloodshed to redeem me.

Now I have wild faith that I have been born part of a network and body called Earth, and that it is by our sweat and blood we will work for redeeming and restoring the harm humanity has inflicted.

I once believed I needed to read and study words collected, decided on, and voted on by men in power to better understand what I called God.

Now I know that as I put my hands in the creek and feel my feet on the pebbles I am living and breathing and getting to know Source.

WE TAKE our kids to meet with our friend Derek and his daughter in the humid dog days of summer. The promises of not just a creek but a cold mountain spring give us hope for some relief. I wade out across the spring-fed water, my feet so cold I start to feel aches in my toes. I carefully step on the rocks beneath me, watching for crawdads, tiny fish, and especially water snakes. Once I reach the point where the waters from the spring mingle with the creek, I feel the coming together of warm and cold, slow and slower still.

I wander into the shallow bed, heading downstream and stand outside the water on a bed of small stones and sandy soil.

I feel as though I'm peering into a portal as I wonder what the rest of the downstream holds, beyond the curve ahead where fewer people are. I see the threshold into the wilder and unknown, but calls of "snake!" draw me back upstream where a small brown water snake has peeked out from a larger rock. Her presence has drawn kids and grown-ups alike, and as we look around, we notice she is not the only one. I look up from where she is suspended upright in the water and notice a clearing in the trees.

As I step out of the creek, cross a footbridge and put my feet on the grass of the clearing, I notice a tree. He is old, worn, and damaged in places. I ask permission and then put my hand on the trunk as I speak words of love and listen. The message is clear. "Come, gather here in this wild place." I say that I will. I promise to return and bring others to gather in the clearing so that they too will know what all I just learned of the Creator and of the spirits among us and of true wild faith.

INVITATION:

I invite you to be outside and to say this "Earth Prayer" which is modeled after what is commonly called "The Jesus Prayer." It is offered here to help connect us with our rootedness in Sacred Unity.

> *Earth, Our Mother*
> *Hold us in all of our wandering*
> *Your Children*

This can also be adapted as a "breath prayer" where the first line is spoken on the inhale, and the second on the exhale.

> *Mother Earth*
> *Hold us*

What do you feel when you speak or meditate on these words? What does it bring up in you that you can do through wild faith?

CHAPTER 24
OUR BODIES, MOTHER EARTH

As AUTUMN BEGINS to make promises of change to come, I take a walk through the pasture beside our house in the mornings. Hay grows tall along the path on which I walk, a one-lane grassy road that leads to my mother-in-law's driveway. Each morning, as the sun rises and catches the dew on the stalks, I notice sagging spiderwebs with hints of gold along their silver threads. The song of wrens and insects intermingle, and the sweet relief of a cooler morning offers me a respite from a long and unnaturally hot summer. I wonder to myself if this is what it was like—that line in Genesis about walking with God in the cool of the day.

In other words, I wonder if this is what it means to commune with Spirit and a close relationship to nature. Then, I began to wonder about other elements of the story of the Garden of Eden, and how we got into this current mess we are in. How might we understand things now?

I reflect on Robin Wall Kimmerer's retelling of the story of Sky Woman and how different this creation story is from the one I came to know as a child. The one I would often return to as I tried to figure out who I am and how a woman who is a lesbian could somehow find a place in the Kin-dom. The story of love and deep connection with the land sits with me more deeply and resonantly than the one of expelling and blaming and "original sin."

I start to ask a new question as I turn around at the end of the path to walk back toward the house on my final lap. What if the story of being cast away from Eden in Genesis is the result of how a particular people long ago were trying to understand the separation so many of us feel? What if this passage is parable for how the pursuit of knowledge and civilization and the so-called advancement of humanity is actually preventing us from true communion and true connection with all of the Divine, including our own divinity? And what if, even if this is not the original thought of the story, this perspective might offer us insight into our current state of being?

I see evidence of the separation all around me. My wife and I take our children to the park to play in the splash pad area. As they run and play around the fountains along with dozens of other kids, we can't help but notice the parents around us. My wife and I, along with a few other brave souls step into the waters with our children. Their sheer delight and unbridled desire for connection and play bring out our own playfulness and wildness. As we sit down to dry off and watch them continue to dance in the water, we notice the many parents not interacting or even watching their kids.

Instead their eyes stay glued to small screens in their hands, their fingers scrolling constantly and only looking up briefly to say "uh-huh, yeah honey," when their children ask if they saw them. I notice how out of breath most of them are even when walking toward their kids to help them on or off of one of the many animal statues in the splash pad.

It saddens me that this is what so many of us have become,

sedentary and tethered to screens. My wife and I talk later about our fears for our generation and the health issues and disconnection plaguing so many. How many will live past 50? How many will have relationships with their children? What kind of relationships will their children be able to have?

Then I wonder how much of it is rooted in belief. I once had a major disagreement with a progressive minister who thought any belief or theological perspective should have a voice and be welcomed equally. But as I said to her, it isn't just about having a voice or being listened to. It's about stopping harm. Correction is necessary.

The same deep spiritual problem which causes us to neglect the body of Mother Earth encourages us to neglect our own bodies. Seeded within the stories and lessons we are taught from the Garden of Eden to the book of Revelations— our physical selves, our bodies, pay dearly for the doctrines of self-abandonment and self-denial. The language of warring between flesh and spirit finds its way into songs, incantations, prayers, and our self-talk. We give up mindful connection and interplay between our spiritual, physical, and emotional parts of ourselves in favor of compartmentalization and the guise of safety and purity. But all of this comes at the cost of the interrelationship and Divine state of being we can experience when we are more fully aware of our wholeness.

Our theologies inform the way we see ourselves, the way we view the world, and the way we view Divine. If we believe "God is not of the world," then it becomes easier to pollute and exploit the Earth. If we believe our bodies are only temporary vessels housing our spirits, then it becomes easier to eat artificial and toxic foods and substances. If we believe our bodies are somehow against our spirits, then a sedentary and disembodied existence may feel more comfortable and safe. If we believe this world is not our home but only a place we travel through, then our bodies and the planet become like a burner account or phone, easily discarded and unprecious to us. And caring about others becomes pointless.

But I know none of these things to be the deep truth.

The deep truth says that we are this Earth. The deep truth says that our bones are made of minerals, our blood of water, and our spirit and life-force the fire as we draw the air around us into our lungs.

> *Earth my body*
> *Water my blood*
> *Air my breath*
> *Fire my spirit*

The ancient chant with mysterious origin reminds us who we are.

All parts of us, our bodies included, are holy and good.

The deep truth is that Spirit is alive in this Earth and in you and I.

We think we know better, but when we have forgotten this deep truth in our never ending pursuit of knowing, we don't know better. We only know worse.

When we begin to awaken to or at least be open to the belief that we are the Earth and that our bodies are good, we start to break free of the reins placed on us by empire and an institutional church who wed itself to empire long ago.

As a queer woman, I especially had a complicated relationship with my body. For all of us who have been taught that who we are is sinful or that our sexuality is broken, we may distrust our bodies even more. That makes reclaiming them even more important and powerful.

Beginning to trust our bodies begins with being in our bodies more. Instead of numbing out and scrolling mindlessly, it means living an embodied presence. There is nowhere that is more attainable than in tandem with the Earth. Through engaging our senses, nature immerses us in the *here* and in the *now*.

Walking along a forest path, I breathe and take in the scents of pine and earthiness. Standing in a creek, I feel the stones under my bare feet and the coolness of the water flowing around my legs. Sitting on the beach, I hear the sounds of ocean waves, gulls, and the breeze. Watching a sunrise, I cannot count all the shades and hues in the sky. A wild ripe blackberry fills my mouth with sweet and tart playing together. All of these call me to be embodied.

Only from this kind of embodied presence can we then do the work of starting to love and trust our physical selves. We might start small, with appreciation and gratitude for each of our senses. We might begin to love the way our bodies allow us to be in the Earth. Then we might begin to trust our sense of sound or sight to protect us. We might trust that we know when it's cold enough for a coat and too hot to be in the full sun. We can recognize this as the wisdom of our bodies.

When we live in our bodies and feel that rootedness with the Earth, we can start to trust our intuition: our gut. And it is listening to our intuition and those little inklings that allows us to recognize and listen to the wisdom of the trees, the water, the wind, and the many more-than-human beings around us.

What would it be like to create our own walking with Spirit in the cool-of-the-day experiences? I invite you to engage in the invitation to connect more deeply to your body as rooted in the natural world.

INVITATION:

For each of these experiences, do what you are able. If you are vision or hearing impaired or have a difficult time with taste or smell, you might wish to modify this and repeat another sense or focus on aspects of the sense that you can safely experience.

Practice being in your body in the Earth with your senses. As you experience each of these, also give gratitude for what you can experience in your body. Thank your body. Thank the Earth.

Sight: Close your eyes for a few moments. As you open them again, pay attention. What colors do you see as your eyes come into focus? What features become more clear as you continue to look? What draws your eyes?

Sound: Close your eyes again and tune your ears to what you hear. Rustling? Birdsong? Insects? Traffic or a train in the distance? Water?

Touch: Place your hands on the ground or in water if you can. Or perhaps you can touch sand, a tree (asking permission from the tree first), or simply notice the temperature. Do you feel a breeze? What does being outside feel like to your body? How does it feel to feel your feet or body on the ground?

Scent: What do you notice with your sense of smell? Evergreen? A leaf bed or fallen pine needles? The dirt? Salt in the air or seaweed? Flowers in bloom or vegetable plants?

Taste: Eat something fresh. It could be a safely and responsibly foraged plant or a conventional fruit or vegetable. What do you taste? What do you notice in your body when you eat food fresh from the Earth? How does it feel in your mouth?

CHAPTER 25
A WILDER DIVINE

SITTING in a college class on the Bible, I remember feeling like something was crashing down around me. I was in my early twenties, and I had just learned about the canonization process for the Bible. I felt like a secret had been held from me, or like I had believed a lie. It would not be the last time a paradigm shift in my perspective occurred, but it was the first domino to fall in my understanding of how institution, patriarchy, whiteness, and empire have convoluted our deep understandings through order-ination, control, suppression, and even violence.

For too many of us, we are unacquainted with how familiar terms, the texts we consider sacred, hymnology, and more have all been weaponized against those considered "outsiders" or people to be controlled. For others of us, we know these patterns all too well. If we are not familiar with the harm toward people who are Indigenous, Black, women, queer, and poor, committed by the church, then we need to familiarize ourselves with a true and unflinching look at history. We must also understand the harm done to the land, the waters, and to life-forms outside of humanity. And we must look with open eyes at the harm being done now in the most recent wave of Christian nationalism.

When we do this, it leaves us with a burning question: if all of this was done in the name of God as we've been taught to know God, what if all of that is based on a misassumption (at best) or (very likely) a lie about who the Divine actually is?

Re-engaging with the wildness around and within us is critical, but that can only take us so far.

What's needed is to realign our spirits with an understanding of the Wild Sacred, the Divine Mystery, a wild and unruly Spirit in between and in all things.

Until we can truly let go of our image of a white male god sitting on a throne, lording and declaring himself king over everything, we can never free ourselves from colonization. Until we can stop using the language of violence, dominion and hierarchy, whiteness and patriarchy, we can never be free from the clutches of those evils, especially when it comes to our language about what many of us call God, or the Divine, or Spirit.

In Christianity, we were often taught to pray what has been labeled by some scholars as a poor translation of Jesus' famous prayer. We revert to speaking archaic language we never use, but cling to the hollowness nevertheless. In the process, we reinforce what we should move away from.

We reinforce a patriarchal distant God. "Our Father who art in heaven."

We reinforce forced worship. "Hallowed be thy name."

We reinforce dominionism. "Thy Kingdom come. Thy will be done. On earth as it is in heaven."

Perhaps most harmfully, we reinforce our own helplessness. We pray "Lead us not into temptation, but deliver us from evil, for thine is kingdom and the power," and in so doing forget and relinquish our own powers of resistance and right-making.

What if we instead delivered *each other* from the evils around us? The evils of violence, hunger, ableism, racism, queerphobia, overconsumption, and more? What if we delivered the *ecosystems* within forests from the evils of clearcutting?

This is a kin-dom, and this kin-dom belongs to each of us. It belongs to me, to you, and also to the trees, the fish, the birds, the insects, the stones, the rivers and oceans, and all. There is no king in the sense we think of kings. No one lording over everyone and everything. Only the interconnection, the Divine dancing among and in us all. The Conversation. The Sacred Wild.

I believe that the margins hold more glimpses of the Divine *because* the Divine is more present with the marginalized, the outside, the uncolonized and decolonized.

What if we imaged the Divine as a queer neurodiverse woman, her arms tattooed like works of art? What if "God" were represented as a Black grandmother with a laughter deep as the wood? An Indigenous elder with hands aged by the sun? The Cailleach (Celtic wise woman) with her mischievous wrinkled grin?

But what if we go even further and begin to see the Divine not as a singular person, but as the *bond* within a relationship, a community, an ecosystem? What if we imagined Spirit as the ocean? From whale sharks and jellyfish to schools of fish to the coral, shells, and plankton to the water itself? What about the entirety of the forest, from the mycorrhizal fungi to the insects, wild berries, the ferns and flowering plants, the mammals, the trees, and the many birds and the scents of pine, cedar, dying leaves, and soil? What if the chorus of birdsong, cicadas, tree frogs, and rustling branches are closer to the sounds of the Sacred than any hymn or song could dare attempt?

I wonder what would shift within us if we started viewing

Divine as a verb. As conversation, as justice-making-organizing, as love between friends, as community building and connections, as the bond between parent and child. How might we then live differently?

I've been captivated for some time over the idea that our concepts of God are too small. But now I've realized through the colonizing, sanitizing, and whitewashing over the past centuries, our idea of God is too tame. Too white. Too male. Too human.

Even in the Bible, there are many examples of a wild Divine: a whirlwind, speaking and nonspeaking animals, dew, a burning bush, fire, a gentle breeze. In the Sacred Wild, we get a glimpse of a holy which is wondrous, powerful, subtle, and in-between.

In Celtic traditions, apples, hazelnuts, salmon, and wells are seen as sources of Divine Wisdom.

If the Divine is wild, then meeting this Wild Holy Spirit would mean getting outside of the small boxes we've built around what counts as worship, as prayer, as spiritual. It would mean many of the ways we've been doing church actually create more distance between ourselves and Spirit. It would mean that our ridiculous attempts are mere noise when we could have been acting justly and doing good for our neighbors and the Earth. It would mean spirituality is not meant to be individual, and honestly? That it even *couldn't* be individual.

Meeting the Wild Divine in Wild Spirituality will draw us out of self-centeredness and into deeper community and kinship.

My dear friend Martha, a retired minister and wonderful feminist and activist, would take walks in the woods with me when she lived nearby. Sometimes, we would laugh. Other times we would cry and cuss. I started admiringly calling our outings "cuss and hikes."

Martha walked with me as I experienced wounding and injustice on a personal level with what happened at our church. At the same time, the 2024 election had just happened, and like many queer folks, my family was reeling in grief and fear.

In the last service I attended and led worship, I was unaware it would be my final Sunday. A lot was happening behind the scenes without my knowledge, and I felt uneasy about the future. But within the first service of the new year, we engaged in spiritual practices including a white stone ceremony, a burning bowl, and remembering our baptism. That day Martha stood by a baptismal and scooped small amounts of water to drip on our foreheads. Though I was already not feeling up for Christian ritual, I knew I wanted Martha to baptize me.

As she sprinkled the water on my forehead, she smiled and spoke the words, that I would always know I belong in the Kin-dom.

This Kin-dom has expanded far beyond what I could have imagined upon leaving the church, feeling alone and deeply betrayed. The Sacred Wild exists in a Kin-dom far beyond what many of us have been able to imagine and beyond our collective harms we've experienced. The Wild Holy Kin-dom is the presence of the Wild Divine Mystery.

When we awaken to the Wild Sacred, we recognize the futility of much religious expression. We quickly see the ways that separateness, hierarchy, formality, and supremacy have warped and erased what our ancestors once knew to be true. Our task then is to work toward restoration and reclaiming a Divine who is wild and untamable. We will need to be open, to expand our views and expressions, yes, but also open to possibilities, to moving and living and loving in rhythms that might be unpredictable and changing and yet constant in their call to participate in the interconnectedness.

We will see the Divine more clearly in each other, in the black bear running through the forest, in the way trees communicate with each other, in the howl of coyotes, and in every hue of green across the land. Perhaps in returning to the Divine as wild, we will then give the Earth the reverence, honor, and care we should in acts of reciprocity and love.

INVITATION:

John Muir once tied himself to a tree to feel the wild power of a storm. He held his head as close to a roaring waterfall as he could. Both of these encounters made him feel closer to the Wild Divine.

While these are obviously dangerous (and I do not recommend them), there are other ways we can remember the wildness of the Divine through natural encounters.

We can observe rapids, a thunderstorm, a bird of prey in flight, but also migrations, still water, the call of loons and crickets, swimming otters and fish, plants growing through concrete. The possibilities are endless.

With a friend or group if possible, or even on your own, go outside and watch with wonder of the wildness. Look deeply for what is untamed. What do you notice about it? What does it teach you about Spirit? Give thanks.

CHAPTER 26
LOVING THE WILD OF THE WORLD AND WITHIN

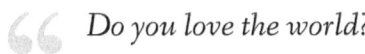 *Do you love the world?*

— *MARY OLIVER*

WHEN I WAS 12 years old, I moved into a new class for my church's Wednesday night services. My family had only been at this church for less than two years, but it was enough time for me to build anticipation for this transition to get to be part of this one teacher's group. Everyone loved her and raved about how much we would all come to adore her, too. I remember being led down the tile hallway into her room and sitting at a table full of other eager middle schoolers.

I don't recall much about that evening's lesson other than two things. First, the woman announced she wouldn't be leading the class anymore and someone else would be taking over soon. Second, she taught a lesson that has stayed with me, but not in a good way. "Never love anything that can't love you back," she spoke as she looked down on us, even though she was seated, too. Someone had said something about loving their pet, and this was her response.

I remember feeling it in my bones, the deep disagreement inside of me. "Of course our pets love us!" I wanted to yell, but I had never felt such disagreement and anger and disillusionment in church before. It certainly wouldn't be the last time. But back then, my muscle of speaking up hadn't been developed or even worked a single time. I still operated under the toxic belief imposed on me as a young southern girl in the church, that I should listen and never talk back. I went home, blood boiling and snuggled our cat and tried to pet our miniature dachshund who hated me.

As the years and decades have gone by, I still think of what this woman's false words might have done. I still bristle at the notion of what she said. And I continue to feel sorry for her and angry at her for saying what she did. I've always known it wasn't true. But what about the other kids in the class?

What about the kids who assumed we can't be loved by animals? What about the kids who grew up to become adults who have difficult relationships and objectify other people into the "can't love me back" category? What about the ones who have never known the love of the Earth, the land, the waters, the old trees who beckon us toward them to come and rest awhile in their shade?

The narratives we are taught while growing up—that we are separate, elevated over, have dominion, or even the seemingly less harmful "stewards"—all create deep wounds and problems which feed into the lack of love for Earth.

The first time I read the poem *Peonies* by Mary Oliver, I immediately fell in love with this poet and her view of Earth and the wonders here. When she asks us, the readers, if we love the world, she poses a question that in many Christian traditions would sound more like an accusation than an invitation.

For too long, church leaders have espoused the idea that loving the world and loving God are opposites. So loving the world might at first feel wrong or even scandalous. Some might suggest seduction and temptation.

But perhaps being drawn in and seduced by nature is exactly what we need in order to remember an unrelenting and wild love. Perhaps coming to know Earth as a compassionate lover who showers us with affection would have the power to change us. Perhaps joining in a reciprocal giving and caring and even expressing romance like that of poets and regenerative gardeners and naturalists would heal the divide we've grown too accustomed to.

Perhaps by loving the world we are in, we might better love the Divine, better love each other, and better love ourselves.

Love requires action, communication, and presence. Loving the world means receiving the gifts and love present in Earth, and love means giving attention, care, and protection. We need to open our hearts to love the world fiercely.

When we love, it makes us willing to fight for and stand for the ones we love. When we are in healing and reciprocal relationships, we naturally want to protect and care for each other.

Sometimes I've wondered what I can possibly do that might be meaningful in caring for Earth. When I see upsetting climate news or habitat destruction, my commitment to being more sustainable and efforts to reduce, reuse, recycle seem like trying to collect water in a sieve.

But then there are days when I look at the dead hedge I created around my garden, and I see the native plants thriving, hear the many pollinators buzzing around, and I know my small acts have made a difference.

It begins with paying attention. In this attention-based economy, choosing to give our attention to the Earth becomes not just a radical act of resistance, but an act of choosing love.

Mysteriously, giving our attention to the Earth tunes us in to the deep connection we have with this planet. We are not just in this world. We *are this Earth.*

But for those of us taught to be in the world and not of it, that truth has been obscured. And as many of us were taught to distrust our own bodies, the Church also taught many of us to distrust our own wildness. Throughout our social structure from workplace to school to religion and even within the home, we are taught to suppress our own wildness. This notion of self shame and self suppression ran deep into my being, earnestly praying for a part of myself, the wild and queer part, to be eradicated.

In the ways we have structured every aspect of our lives around capitalism and productivity, our natural inclinations and instincts suffer from a lack of engagement. In the ways we've instituted hierarchical rule and order, our *own* knowing, wisdom, and authority take a backseat to what we choose to follow instead.

But what if we were to realize that *we are the Sacred Wild,* and grow to love the wild within ourselves?

Through the fog of a misty rain, my family pulled into Crawford Notch State Park in the White Mountains of New Hampshire. My friends Jess and Corey had recommended we visit the park as we stayed with them. It was October, and the golds of paper birch and maples sang out among the firs and spruces. Their reflections echoed across the lake. I couldn't take my eyes off of the mountainside and water, the way they touched and called out to me.

As my family walked across a footbridge and into the forest, a deep hush fell over me. At times I didn't know whether to be still, to go further in, or to reach out and explore the boulders of granite, the lichens, and the branches reaching down to the paths. While in the White Mountains, we walked on the stone floor near waterfalls, climbed up mountainsides, and exchanged air with trees that don't grow in the Southeast.

Somehow I couldn't find words for the sacredness I felt, the way I connected with something both larger than me and something within me. On the way home, we listened to a podcast episode with Valarie Kaur talking to Brené Brown. In it, Valarie talked about meeting strangers and recognizing others as parts of us we have not met yet. I recognized in that moment what I had encountered. In our travels to some of the wilds of New Hampshire and Vermont, I met a part of Source and a part of me I had not met yet. It left me breathless and awestruck.

When I witness and appreciate the rush of a waterfall, I can feel appreciation for the way I also spill over and flow. When I know the steadiness and slow growth of a tree, I can love the way I can weather storms and dry seasons. When I love the way blackberries grow wherever the hell they want to, I open myself to love the ways I show up as a marginalized person. When I laugh in delight at a group of ducks quacking, I love my own silliness. When I tear up at the beauty of the sandhill cranes migration overhead, I love the way it feels in my body to be in community.

Our wildness may have been suppressed, but our wildness is still living, as close as our breath. Releasing our fear—of being outside of what a religion taught us or being too silly or being seen as too different—releases our sacred wild selves from the confinements built by empire.

> *I am sacred. I am wild.*
> *I am Earth and Heaven's child.*
> *I am sacred. I am wild.*

When we raise our voices and move our bodies and place our hands in the Earth and in the water, we know.

I am free and I am whole
In my body and my soul.
I am sacred. I am wild.

When we love our own sacred wildness and realize we are the Earth, we awaken to the sacred wildness of our neighbors, both human and more-than-human. We awaken to the sacred wild in all, and we begin to love with attention, care, protection, and justice-making.

Loving the wild of the world and within is not a call to more individualism. It is a commission to be an intentional part of the web of life, to invest in community, and to love all others and ourselves fiercely and actively.

I TAKE a walk outside on another dew-soaked morning. As I walk outside the door, I instantly recognize I have crossed a threshold. The cries of two hawks beckon me further up the hill and into the Sacred Wild. I am surrounded by bird and insect song as the sun plays upon the dewdrops on the plants below. My eyes catch a shimmer in the distance, sunlight playing on the feathers of a flock of wild turkeys in the distance. I continue to walk on, but soon understand I should go another way when I notice a small bird wary of me. I turn so she can be more at peace.

As I walk in a different direction, a locust flies up and glitters in the morning sun, appearing blue and purple, even though when he lands I can see he is brown and spotted. I walk away from him, too, and stand pondering the question: "What is alive for me in this moment?" The cackling of a pileated woodpecker echoes in the air, and I take in a deep breath. Then my eyes are drawn to the dew. Instead of taking off my shoes, I crouch and put my hands on the ground. I can't believe the diversity and variety all around. Then I notice a single silver drop hanging from a blade of grass. I reach down so my hand is beneath and pull my hand back toward me, the drop suspended on my skin, making me shimmer.

I don't overthink what comes next. I know it's been coming. I just didn't think it would happen here, with this tiny drop, in my own backyard. I thought it would be a waterfall that would call to me for this moment, but here it calls me, in the everyday morning dew.

I take the drop and place it on my forehead. I draw a circle.

I am baptized by the Sacred Wild.

I speak it. I commit myself to love and care and to witness Spirit in all. I feel Mother Earth's pulse beneath my hands. Words form on my lips from my heart: "Bone of my bone, spirit of my spirit, I am you. We are connected, and I will care for you and love you and honor your sacredness and Spirit in you."

I take more dew drops on my hands and draw another circle in silence, then I wash my hands in the grass and clover.

When I come back inside and cross back into the room where I am writing and editing, I know I've crossed another threshold. I think of the words of Irish poet John O'Donahue about threshold and the act of threshing. All that is left now is indeed the grain.

INVITATION:

In opening your heart to loving the Wild of the world and within, you must connect with the realization that you are the Earth, too.

Outside, in a place that is meaningful or beautiful to you, place your feet or hands on the ground. You can be sitting, or you can lie on the ground.

What do you feel beneath you? Close your eyes if that helps you tune in more deeply.

Recognize this Earth pulse in the tiny tremors, in the way life teems around and beneath you, and within the beating of your own heart. Place one of your hands on your chest as you continue to sense the pulse of the Earth. Imagine or recognize they are deeply connected, tuned in to each other and echoing back and forth in conversation.

You are sacred. You are wild. You are Earth and Heaven's child.

This connection is holy and good, and the more you return to this connection, the deeper your love and actions that support that love will grow.

After you have connected, take some time to listen to what the Earth and what Spirit ask of you. What small actions can you take? What systems can you influence? How can you show up in love?

CHAPTER 27

NATURAL INTELLIGENCE

IT IS NOT LOST on me that as I've been writing this book on eco-spirituality and nature, there has been an explosion of AI. Artificial intelligence has infiltrated many areas of society from healthcare to publishing to news and even using ChatGPT as a trusted confidant. I would be lying to you if I told you I had any sort of open mind toward generative AI. As an artist and writer, I know firsthand the violation of having work stolen to train it. As a person with a strong background in mental health and well-being, I see real and present dangers. As a person who loves this planet, I cannot abide the pollution, water usage, and habitat destruction that power AI data centers.

The way AI has begun to warp our sense of shared reality should give concern to us all. AI created videos and pictures become more realistic and bring questions of what is real vs. what is fabricated. But another and perhaps more sinister danger lurks with the ways AI is being used to create artificial relationships from chatbots to AI controlled stuffed animal companions.

What are we doing here?

As AI continues to replace people who used to perform jobs or replace the role of a trusted friend for processing something with, I keep coming back to the same line of thought.

What about lived experience that leads to wisdom?

What about embodiment?

What about true relationship with humans, plants, and animals?

What about natural intelligence?

In the race to have the best version of AI, it seems like much of Western society is forgetting the fact there is already technology available to make our lives better. There is already in place, a system for improving our moods, our knowledge, and our relationships. In fact, it's old technology that does not need new gadgets or "smart" devices. Natural intelligence.

We were once way-finders. People could navigate the seas by using the stars as their guides. Civilizations knew how to navigate rivers and traverse mountains and deserts without even a compass or map. Now some of us can't find a friend's house without pulling their address up in our phones, even if we've visited several times.

We were once healers. Modern medicine has done wonders for our longevity and quality of life, and we should be incredibly grateful for it. But where many of our ancestors knew what foods and herbs would help create more health and wellbeing and even offer healing, we grab fast foods, ignore nutrition, and hope the medications we take will make up for our unhealthy lifestyles.

We were once freer and more able to learn the skills of ancestors and have more time to take care of our bodies, but many of us have been shackled by labor systems under a brutal form of capitalism that only serves those at the top.

We used to have the collective wisdom and insight of our

neighbors, our villages, our clans and relatives. Now we turn to search engines and AI chat programs.

If we were to return to natural intelligence, could we counter-balance the misinformation, the destruction, and the deep loneliness of our time?

In restoring our relationship to the land and waters and restoring our spirits to wildness, reclaiming this kind of wisdom empowers us to reject artificial living. We can, instead, collectively move toward a more natural and sustainable way to live.

How do we begin to restore our natural intelligence when both the separation and the wheel of empire have taken so much?

Reacquainting ourselves to our more-than-human neighbors offers us a great place to start. Getting to know the names of what birds are singing outside of our homes and what little plants and trees grow where we live help inch us closer to relationship. Noticing what spiders weave their webs and what birds nest on our shrubs and porches reminds us who else call this "home." Asking a tree for permission to touch her and waiting for the response reminds us of the sentience and rights of beings we've often dismissed. Treating a stone in a way that is kind recognizes the pulsating energy present there, captured in the Celtic St. Patrick's prayer rewritten by George MacLeod.

Natural intelligence also includes a return to the silence and the darkness. Quiet places and dark skies become increasingly rare due to noise and light pollution. We can no longer hear grass blow in the wind or see the Milky Way from most places within the U.S., and indeed many places on Earth. Many stars have become obscured, and even if we knew the skills of the way finders in our ancestry, we could often not even see what we need to guide us home. New satellites create more chaos and obscure the star patterns. What guides us home has been obscured by what we've misidentified as important or as home.

The darkness has become vilified. This vilification spills over into racism and colorism as we equate darkness with something wrong or to be feared. It spills over into light pollution galore as we think of darkness as something to be fixed or snuffed out.

What if we remembered that darkness is a friend, the womb, the deep soil in which life and knowing incubate?

What if we worked to rewild our night skies by cutting out light pollution and even taking steps like some cities in the world to become dark sky sanctuaries?

What would we then see if we removed the cloak of artificial light and peered into the darkness as it reveals the wonder of stars, planets, and our place in the universe?

Similarly, silence has become a void to fill with noise, scrolling, and mindless chatter. The filling of this void has stolen boredom, patience, and understanding.

What if we returned to viewing silence as rest, a moment to go deeper, an opportunity to breathe and simply be?

What if we restored and protected quiet places and worked to cut out noise pollution and did our part to restore natural quiet?

Could we hear the heartbeat of the Earth? Could we once again know what birds are singing and recognize the sound of the wind blowing across a field, rustling the grass and flowers? Would we remember what it's like to wonder in silence?

As the pressure to separate from the natural world and even reality becomes greater, our need to restore our natural intelligence will only grow.

I sometimes wish I could go back in time and ask my grandfather and great-grandmother about the moon signs and living by them. I sometimes wish I could travel back to my Celtic ancestors and find out what plant and Earth wisdom they might share. Sometimes I long to have some kind of written record from my ancestors for what they might have known and trusted about being alive in the Earth.

But no matter how many books I read or how many conversations I have, there comes a point when natural intelligence must be *embodied*. While AI can spew facts and lies and repeat what it's learned from humans, only a lived experience embodied in Earth can give us the deepest truths.

This knowing in our bones, feeling it in our blood, recognizing it in the air, trusting it in our hearts kind of intelligence comes from our lived humanity. This wisdom cannot be bought or sold, but it can be lost if we continue to atrophy.

Can it be restored? I believe so.

We begin to restore our natural intelligence when we choose to be present in our bodies. We restore it through engaging our senses in the Wild, taking in what we can and recognizing our kinship. We restore it when we listen and hear what the Earth is telling us. We restore it when we are present with other people, recognizing them as kin within the Earth. We restore it when we choose to call a friend instead of asking ChatGPT to process something with us. We restore it when we pay attention to our surroundings and commit to memorizing our way. We restore it when we offer gratitude and honor to the beings living where we do, sharing our home.

We restore our natural intelligence when we learn the skills of those who have gone before us and commit ourselves to living closer to the Earth, embodied and full of wonder. When we trust our guts. When we listen and embrace Earth-based cultural wisdom. When we walk through the world, knowing we are kin. And when we stop turning to technology for knowledge, insight, and companionship.

Intimacy and erotic intelligence expert Esther Perel sometimes asks audiences how many of them woke up and touched their phone first thing in the morning. She then will ask how many of them did that with a person next to them. I wonder how many of us have the light of a screen touch our eyes before the light of the sun or moon. I wonder how many of us touch a phone or device before our skin meets the air outside, much less our feet on the ground. How often do we watch and listen to a video on social media before we hear birdsong?

How much more intimate and intelligent would our relationship with the world be if even these small changes were taken to heart? Perhaps this is the place to begin in restoring our natural intelligence. One day and one wakening at a time.

INVITATION:

When you wake up, set the intention to not touch your phone until you have experienced morning light, listened to bird song, or at least felt the air outside. What do you notice when you begin your day this way instead? What is challenging about it?

What other ways of natural intelligence do you want to embrace? Would you like to be more intentional to connect directly with friends and call them instead of asking Chat GPT? Would you like to pay more attention and learn to navigate? Perhaps a skill calls to you that you would like to learn. As legendary conservationist Jane Goodall said in a final interview, when we make small changes collectively, they add up into a big change and make a difference. Imagine how much difference could be made if we all embraced more natural intelligence.

Discuss this with others in your life. Don't keep it a secret. Encourage other people you know and are in relationship with to embrace natural intelligence.

CHAPTER 28
WILD GEESE

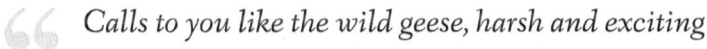 *Calls to you like the wild geese, harsh and exciting*

— *MARY OLIVER*

FOR SEVERAL YEARS, anytime I found myself in a spot where I needed hope or faced a big transition in my life, hawks would appear to me. One landed in a tree outside my office window when a band member called to tell me he was moving away. The moment I reached the pinnacle of my loneliness and despair in my own coming out process, a hawk flew and called out overhead.

In the 2011 super outbreak of tornadoes, a twister touched down in my neighborhood, leaving electrical wires and trees all over the ground and my system stunned by the trauma of it all. My dear friend, Sarah, and I walked hand-in-hand after she stayed the night comforting me. Three hawks circled in the air, their loud cries echoing above the wreckage.

I realized only recently that another bird has entered my life to offer messages and knowing when I needed it most. On

Sept. 1, 2021, I stepped outside one morning, deeply sad and feeling lonely. Sarah, that dear friend who at this point had become more like a sister, had called me a couple weeks before to tell me she was moving across the country. Tears in my eyes and lump in my throat, I stood outside with our dog, Maple. The change of seasons whispered in the breeze as the morning light started breaking through. Then they came flying over-head. A small flock of wild geese.

Over the years, they have continued to come to me. Harbin-gers of change, shifting, and the need to move. Wisdom bearers of migration and knowing when it's time.

I sit on the back porch in the waning heat of summer and have a conversation with Aline over the phone. We spend most of the talk discussing our projects, processing recent experiences, and offering support to each other's plans and aspirations. But then she asks me a simple question, some-thing about music and church, and the leadership role I had taken on and the commitment it required of my time and energy.

I hadn't planned on talking much about where I had been finding myself spiritually, but it comes spilling out anyway. In the form of out-loud wonderings and longings, I say I am not sure if I want to continue or if I do, how much. I tell her I feel like I have entered into a new season or stage spiritually, that something has shifted deeply within me.

"It's like another crisis of faith," I say a little tentatively then take a breath. "Only... it doesn't feel like a crisis. It feels more like I've outgrown something, and I don't know why I keep trying to fit myself back down into it."

For much of writing this book, I have realized I am in a new place spiritually. I realize that while I have known the language and culture of Christianity for all of my life up to this point, that there is a deep longing for something deeper, freer, and wider. I long for unboundedness like what I see in the Sacred Wild.

I've come to recognize within myself that the label of Christian doesn't fit anymore, and that there is no longer even a desire to make it work. I also see that I still appreciate and honor the way modeled by the person of Jesus. Even though I no longer believe in a need for a savior, I do believe he showed us a beautiful way to live. I once thought the more expanded view of Christ, articulated by Christian mystic and writer Richard Rohr and others might fit. I find beauty in that, but it still makes me hesitate—this language that has done so much harm and taken so much. The echoes of colonization, empire, and demonization of many cultures haunt me.

I sometimes wonder if it's the mere words "Christ" and the related "Christian" that have come to repel me in some way, especially in the rise of Christian nationalism and especially after providing so much trauma work and witnessing and experiencing so much harm myself. Maybe the concept would appeal to me more without that baggage or with different wording. To be honest, I'm not sure.

What I am sure of is that I am beginning to understand that it is not the label or categorizing that matters. That kind of sorting and compartmentalizing are for empire and institutional religion. What I'm most interested in is *living*.

I find myself captivated by how acts of everyday living are deeply spiritual. I gravitate toward spiritual practices and magic creating that are simple, embodied, and present ways to live. From letting my feet be soaked in the morning dew to listening to bird and insect songs to preparing food from the garden, every moment offers a chance to be here and to acknowledge the deep connection of all.

Prayer has become walking, listening, holding questions and asking them. Repentance has metamorphosed into learning what actions and habits I have which cause harm and changing my behavior and working on my attitude. Discipleship has been molded into the deep work of decolonizing myself through listening to voices attuned to Earth, reclaiming my own Earth-connected lineage, and embracing wildness. Spiritual community has expanded beyond what I knew as church and opened to a true field of possibilities amongst the forest, the rivers, the mountains and trees. Worship has become recognizing the worth inherent in all beings, no matter how small, even in the dirt.

While, in some ways, it feels like I have been migrating to a new land spiritually and even physically, my heart tells me I've simply stepped outside.

My soul experiences this as homecoming and deep remembrance, but also way-making.

Stepping outside of what I've known in the church has opened my eyes to what the institution has taken me away from — what my animal body knows and loves. Treading into the waters and upon the rocky mountainsides of wild spirituality has reminded my legs what it feels like to answer the call to adventure. Though too much of my life has been spent following the way the church taught, I feel as if I'm finally falling into step with a way that feels even more sacred, more whole, and maybe even more fully in the way of Jesus that had once captivated me.

Wild geese have not just been a special symbol to me because of their appearance to me when I need them, but also because of the Mary Oliver poem and bedtime stories we've read to our children. In these, wild geese are harbingers of belonging and remembering how loved we are.

Through all of the pain I've experienced by the church, from the spiritual trauma and abuse for being a gay woman to mistreatment and abandonment to the subtle blades of dogma

and theology that tried to cut me away from who I really am—
the deep belonging I've felt in the Wild has remained.

As I've worked to reconnect with my Celtic roots and
understand Earth connection and perspective of Earth as
sacred, I learned the significance of the wild goose in Celtic
mysticism. The early Celtic Christians symbolized Spirit in the
form of the wild goose because these geese are unpredictable
and will not be tamed.

I look around at the Western church imbued with empire
and the control and dominance in the expression of Christian
nationalism. I look at much of the mainline church and the
prescriptive elements, the unimaginative liturgies and death
grip on hymns that also sing of dominion and Christian
supremacy. I look at the ways so many of us: queer, artists,
dreamers, activists, outsiders, and edge-walkers have been
ostracized, demonized, and ultimately rejected by the Church
in many forms.

Then I hear the call of the wild geese high in the sky, the
cry of Spirit to remember our true belonging. I see the migration forming Vs upon Vs, and feel the wind tousle my hair
when the flock flies just overhead, the beating of wings
pulsating in my body and enlivening my breath.

I do not know what the future holds for a church I sometimes wish would just disappear.

I do not know what kind of future an institution that has
wed itself to everything that stands against the way of Jesus and
the way of the Earth even *can* or *should* have. I do know,
though, that beyond church is community and embodiment. I
know that I long for this wildness, and I am not the only one
working to create spiritual community outside of what we've
known as church.

I have a suspicion that Spirit is up to something. I have a
hunch that over the next decades more will release the tired

versions of inauthentic worship, the institutional ways of knowing Divine, and the prescriptive and domineering forms of being in spiritual community.

I have a vision for spiritual gathering and relating and community building outside of capitalism, outside of traditions that do not work, outside of every kind of wall of our own making. I have a vision that more spiritual gatherings and communities will transform in these ways and that spirituality will expand, become more open, and be centered on creation and justice making. I envision a future where wild churches, forest churches, and even indoor churches that adopt a wilder approach will foster kinship and connection where separateness and isolation have infected our communities. I have a vision where no supremacy culture remains, and in its stead we embrace a kinship view.

I long for this kind of approach, where labels do not matter. Where there is no in or out. Where we recognize the interconnection of all. Where inter-spirituality and inter-being infuse our daily lives from how we speak to our children, partners, and friends to how we grow and prepare food and how we spend our money and time. Where we do justice and make peace. Where we build worlds of multiculturalism and equity and Earth restoration. Where we do not look to books and teachers from hundreds of years ago or to a singular person giving a sermon to know more about the Divine.

Where, instead, we put our feet into creek beds and rivers, place our hands on rocks, take in the scents of cedar and pine, and listen to the cries of sandhill cranes and cicadas to better know Spirit. Where we hear the cry of Spirit to come further up and further into the Sacred Wild. Knees, hands, or feet in the dirt of a garden or forest floor. Dirt Church. Where we recognize *the joy of Divine Mystery is all around*. And we embrace a new way to live.

Wild Spirit, come.

IT'S EARLY MORNING. *I am on my walk, just as the sun is starting to hint at rising. Heavy dew drops hang from the hay that wasn't cut, and spider webs shine against the early pinkish light. My boots slog upon the ground, heavy and soaked through. I can smell the earth, and the sharpness of the scent of wet hay opens my senses even more. I'm full of thought until something comes behind me, something loud and wind-like. I turn just in time to see the flock fly just over me. The Wild Geese, fourteen of them or so, flapping as they come over the hill. I can barely breathe or believe it as they go just above the trees ahead of me.*

Just as I start to wonder where they are heading and wonder about their migration, they honk and turn - not just anywhere, but back toward me!

This time, I don't care how water sloshes from my heavy boots. I don't care how hard it is to run. I head up the hill as fast as my feet will take me. As they come back over my head in their holy wild wondrous wing beating, I feel the rush of being caught up. The wings are beating in my own chest. I raise my arms in the rising golden sun.

And I remember: I am wild.

DIRT CHURCH HYMNS

You can find recordings of these songs at my website: charitymmuse.com Please listen along and sing them in community and alone!

I Am Sacred, I Am Wild

> I am sacred. I am wild
> I am earth and heaven's child
> I am sacred. I am wild.
> In my body and my soul
> I am free and I am whole.
> I am sacred. I am wild.
>
> Yea-ah-aaayy!
> Yea-ah-aaayy!

My Body

> My body is good

My body is free
My body is wise
My body is me

The Joy of Divine Mystery

This joy (this joy)
In the morning (in the morning)
Rising on the wind and wings of birds

This joy (this joy)
In the morning (in the morning)
Rising on the song of beloved Earth

Hallelujah (Hallelujah)
She is here (She is here)
Hallelujah (Hallelujah)
It's becoming clear (It's becoming clear)

From the Sacred (From the Sacred)
Holy Ground (Holy Ground)

The joy of Divine Mystery is all
    around
The joy of Divine Mystery is all
    around

For Every Creature

For every creature
For every tree
For every mountain
The rivers and the sea

For every life form
For every being
For every creature
May I bring

Justice, mercy, kindness and healing
May I move from my complacency
To justice, mercy, kindness, and
    healing
For every creature, for every tree

I Open

I am open to the Spirit
I am open to the Wild
I am open to the Spirit
I am open to the Wild

I open
I open
My heart

BIBLIOGRAPHY &
RECOMMENDED READING

Newell, John Phillip. *Sacred Earth, Sacred Soul: Celtic Wisdom for Reawakening to What Our Souls Know and Healing the World*. Harper One, 2021.

Loorz, Victoria. *Church of the Wild: How Nature Invites Us into the Sacred*. Broadleaf Books, 2021.

Loorz, Victoria and Valerie Luna Serrels. *Field Guide to Church of the Wild*. Broadleaf Books, 2025.

Kimmerer, Robin Wall Braiding Sweetgrass: Indigenous Wisdom, Scientific Knowledge, and the Teaching of Plants. Milkweed Editions, 2013.

O Donahue, John. *To Bless the Space Between Us: A Book of Blessings*. Convergent Books, 2008.

Oliver, Mary. *New and Selected Poems*. Beacon Press, 1992.

Lockwood, Devi. *1,001 Voices On Climate Change: Everyday Stories of Flood, Fire, Drought, and Displacement from Around the World*. Simon & Schuster, 2021.

RESOURCES

Websites/Advocacy/Community:

Dark Sky International https://darksky.org

Quiet Parks https://www.quietparks.org

Indigenous Worldview Literacy Project https://worldviewliteracy.org

Center for Spirituality in Nature https://www.centerforspiritualityinnature.org

The Work That Reconnects Network https://workthatreconnects.org (Joanna Macy's work)

The Lost Words https://www.thelostwords.org/

Neil Douglas Klotz (Abwoon) https://abwoon.org

White Supremacy Culture https://www.whitesupremacyculture.info

Keep America Beautiful (Find your local Chapter) https://kab.org/affiliate-look-up/

Interfaith Power and Light Chapters (There are chapters in 40 states and DC)

Nature Conservancy https://www.nature.org/en-us/

Wild Church Network https://www.wildchurchnetwork.com

Plant Baby Plant https://plantbabyplant.com

Kids for Saving Earth https://kidsforsavingearth.org/

Wild Goose Festival https://wildgoosefestival.org

Self-Compassion Institute: https://self-compassion.org/ (Work of Kristin Neff)

RESOURCES

Socially Responsible Agriculture Project https://sraproject.org/

Revolutionary Love Project https://revolutionarylove.org/

Nature Apps:
Seek by iNaturalist
Star Chart
Merlin Bird ID

Your local library is a fantastic resource for field guides, local history, and local watershed ecology.

A "living" resource page for this book can be found on my website: charitymmuse.com It will continue to have additions to these resources.

ACKNOWLEDGMENTS

Creating this book was transformative for me, and I am ever grateful to those who helped me bring this work into the world.

Cass, thank you for creating such a stunning piece of art for the cover. You truly captured my vision and the heart of this book.

Devi, thank you for helping me make this book stronger with your editing suggestions. And thank you for the inspiration to adventure!

Deb and Kyle, thank you for being honest and thorough beta readers. Your feedback helped me know what was the most meaningful within this book and helped it become better. Deb, thank you for also being such a champion for my work in the world.

To the Wild Church Network, especially Valerie: I am so grateful to have found this community. Thank you for encouraging me to go deeper still and for all of the support and guidance in forming our own wild spiritual community.

Beth Remmes, thank you for your beautiful review of this book and for all of your support and encouragement to me!

Beth Norcross, I'm so grateful for your work in this world and for your kindness toward me. Thank you for cheering me on!

Steve, Martha, Naomi, Aline, thank you for your friendship and for journeying with me in my rewilding. I love you all.

Wild Goose Festival, thank you for giving me a place to stretch my own wings.

To the lands, waters, and more-than-humans who shaped my thought, held me in my own rewilding, and beckoned me to come further up and into the wild—I honor you.

Wild Wood Gathering, wild love and gratitude for you all.

Betty Woomer, I will never write a book without thanking you for believing in sixteen-year-old me, especially when I wanted to give up in the face of failure or being told "no." You remain my greatest teacher.

D, thank you for reading and re-reading as I put my thoughts to words. More than that, I'm so glad to do life with you and thankful for how we've grown together. Willow and Sycamore, thank you for embracing this Earth and for the ways you inspire me. I love our family.

To my readers, thank you. You are sacred and wild.

ABOUT THE AUTHOR

Charity Muse is an eco-spiritual facilitator and guide with a background in mental health, higher education, and ministry. She holds a Master's of Science in Mental Health Counseling and is credentialed as a professional coach. She has extensive experience in working with spiritual trauma and training others to do the work. Charity is also a singer/songwriter, and her first novel *Broken to Belong* was published in 2022. She currently resides in Georgia with her wife and kids. Charity facilitates a small eco-spiritual community as part of the Wild Church Network.

You can learn more about Charity and find her music and eco-spiritual work at charitymmuse.com

ALSO BY CHARITY MUSE

Broken to Belong (a novel)

For singer/songwriter Dani Williams, music has always carried her –
until now. No longer able to ignore her pain, Dani travels south to
volunteer at a safe home for LGBTQ+ youth. While there, she meets
Mae, an advisor to the residents whose warmth is contrasted by
guardedness and uncertainty. Dani and Mae form a special bond
which blossoms into love.

But more than their relationship becomes threatened when an attack
is launched against the home, endangering its existence. To help save
the home and the authentic love she yearns for, Dani must face
heartbreak from her past and use her talents to confront the same
prejudice that wounded her. As the strength of their bond is tested,
Dani has the choice to walk away and lose everything or stay and
redefine love, family, and spirit.

Broken to Belong explores what it means to fight for one another and
dares to ask – **can we find or create belonging** where we least
expect it?